B.C

THE EPISTLE TO THE ROMANS

THE EPISTLE
TO THE ROMANS

Theological Meditations

KARL HERMANN SCHELKLE

HERDER AND HERDER

1964
HERDER AND HERDER NEW YORK
232 Madison Avenue, New York 16, N.Y.

Translated from *Meditationen über den Römerbrief*
(Benziger Verlag, Einsiedeln) by Brian Thompson.

Nihil obstat: Patrick A. Barry
                 Censor Librorum

Imprimatur: ✠Robert F. Joyce
                 Bishop of Burlington
                 February 24, 1964

The nihil obstat and imprimatur are official declarations that a
book or pamphlet is free of doctrinal or moral error. No implication is contained therein that those who have granted the nihil
obstat and imprimatur agree with the contents, opinions or statements expressed.

The Epistle to the Romans reprinted from *The New Testament*,
translated by James A. Kleist S.J. and Joseph I. Lilly C.M., 1956,
with the permission of The Bruce Publishing Company,
Milwaukee.

Library of Congress Catalog Card Number: 64–19735
© 1964 by Herder and Herder, Incorporated
Printed in the United States of America

CONTENTS

FOREWORD

No one will dispute the fateful role played by the letter of St. Paul to the Romans in the history of Christianity. St. Augustine felt compelled to pick up the epistle and to read (13:13–14): ". . . Put on the Lord Jesus Christ, and take no thought for your lower nature to satisfy its lusts." And his conversion dated from that time. The importance of Romans, with its emphasis on the "righteousness of God," for the Reformers, such as Luther, Melanchthon and Calvin (of the three only Luther did not write a commentary upon it), is known to all. At Aldersgate Street in the London of 1738 John Wesley came to a new understanding of the letter by way of Luther's preface to it, and he had the heartwarming experience that Christ was his salvation. In more recent times the commentary (1918, and successive editions) of the Swiss theologian Karl Barth has made history. His book is, however less an exegesis of the epistle than an exposition of the theological approach for which he had become famous.

Among Catholic scholars the exegesis of Romans has experienced a renewal since the time of Père Marie-Joseph Lagrange O.P., who wrote a first-class commentary on it in 1916. Lucien Cerfaux of the University of Louvain published a small guide to the epistle in 1949 and explained the

thought of Saint Paul in several other works. Stanislaus
Lyonnet S.J., of the Pontifical Biblical Institute in Rome,
is responsible for many studies on the meaning of God's
justice, and on the meaning of sin (Romans 5:12ff), and
he published a revision of the Huby commentary in 1957.
From Germany has come the commentary of Otto Kuss, of
the University of Munich, and now, in English dress, this
volume by Father Karl Hermann Schelkle, professor of
New Testament in the Catholic theological faculty of the
University of Tübingen.

Father Schelkle's renown as a New Testament scholar is
enough to assure us that this book is more than a mere collection of pious thoughts. It is true that he does away with
the learned apparatus which is usually associated with com-
mentaries, but this work is a straightforward and clear explanation of St. Paul's thought. One might almost say that
the meditations are those of Paul, so closely does Father
Schelkle adhere to the literal sense of the epistle. His purpose is to introduce the reader to the meaning, and thus
induce him to make his own the word that Paul has written. And this letter of Paul is richly deserving of deep meditation, since it contains so much of his own theology: the
saving justice of God, the sinfulness of man, redemption in
Christ, the mystery of Israel.

Karl Barth once wrote: "Am Römerbrief lernt man eben
nicht aus"—"You cannot exhaust the meaning of the letter
to the Romans." Father Schelkle's meditations will greatly
help the reader to sound the depths of a challenging epistle
that is more a theological treatise than it is a letter.

ROLAND E. MURPHY O. CARM.

Author's Note

The English translation of the present work was prepared after the second German edition (1963). The German edition was in several cases supplemented and revised for the translation.

Karl Hermann Schelkle

Tübingen, January 1964

INTRODUCTION

1 PAUL, ROME AND THE ROMAN CHURCH

The apostle Paul's third long missionary journey, probably in the years 53–57, led him from Antioch through Asia Minor (where he spent three years in Ephesus) to Europe and finally to Greece (Acts 18:23—20:3). Paul spent the winter of 57–58 in Corinth, where he lived in the spacious house of Gaius, whom he himself had baptised (1 Cor 1:14). Gaius offered the hospitality of his house to Paul and the whole congregation (16:23).

Since long trips were impossible in the winter Paul used the time to give the church in Corinth stable administration and discipline. The church would thus be safeguarded against disorder and confusion even in the absence of its founding apostle. But Paul's thoughts were traveling forward and backward through time and space. In how many places had he preached during his twenty years of missionary work! In how many places had he founded congregations and strengthened them time and time again! First in Damascus, then in Tarsus, then with Barnabas and the others in Antioch. From Antioch he had undertaken the first missionary journey to Cyprus and southern Asia Minor. The second journey led him further and further through Asia Minor. Then, called by a vision in a dream, he crossed over to Europe and founded churches in Macedonia and Greece. He was also repeatedly in Jerusalem in spite of many obstacles. After Paul, on the third missionary journey through Asia and Europe, had strengthened the old congregations and founded new ones, he was able to say: "From Jerusalem, and in all directions as far as Illyricum, I have fully preached the gospel of Christ . . . But now I have no further field of action in these parts" (15:19–23).

Paul therefore seeks new scope. He is sixty years old. His body, weak by nature, bears the traces of the anxieties, toils and battles of the apostolic ministry. But he can pay no attention to that. He knows that God's strength will be made perfect in his weakness (2 Cor 12:9). The apostle's plans are now directed toward the far west, toward Spain. There the many Roman settlements and the Hellenic culture spread throughout the coastal cities should offer him the possibility of working effectively. Paul wants to travel to Spain via Rome (15:23f). His plans and thoughts have long been directed toward Rome for he is aware of the power and importance of the city. The Acts of the Apostles also testifies to the desires and aspirations of the apostle. In 19:21 we read that Paul intends to travel from Ephesus through Greece to Jerusalem, and says to himself: "After I have been there, I must also visit Rome." In Acts 23:11 Paul is a prisoner in the stronghold Antonia in Jerusalem. The Lord appears to him at night and says: "Be steadfast, for just as you have borne witness to me in Jerusalem, so also must you bear witness in Rome." Jerusalem and Rome are here mentioned in the same breath. They are the City of God and the City of the Emperor. They are the poles, around which the history of the world revolves. They are already, and remain forever, the two capital cities of Christianity.

Paul regarded Rome as the political center of the world. If he sought the centers of commerce and life at all he could not bypass Rome. And since he had the mission to preach the gospel among the Gentile nations this had to take place also in Rome. Therefore he must bear witness in Rome. But it was not easy to preach the gospel of the Crucified One in this particular place. Less than a century before M. Tullius Cicero, the leading statesman of his time, spoke in the Roman Forum, the very center of the city and of the entire empire, at the trial of a Roman governor accused of having Roman citizens crucified in his province, and laid down a principle which still applied in Paul's time: "Whatever may even be called a cross should remain distant not only from the body of Rome's citizens, but even from their thoughts, their eyes, their ears." It is an offense against propriety to even talk about a death as disgraceful as that of a slave upon the cross in the presence of respectable people. But it was precisely here in Rome where the gospel of the cross had to be preached.

Paul was not permitted to visit Rome and the Roman community, as he hoped to according to the Epistle to the Romans. From Corinth he traveled early in 58 first of all and once more to Jerusalem. There his destiny was fulfilled. The opposition of the Jews united against him. They saw in Paul a traitor to their people for he maintained that the promises and salvation of God pass from the Jews to the Gentiles (Acts 21–23). The Roman tribune in Jerusalem protected Paul against persecution, assault and even violent death by taking him into protective custody (Acts 23:10). For two years, 58–60, Paul had to remain under detention, pending investigation (Acts 23–25). Then the apostle demanded that since he was a Roman citizen he be brought before the imperial court in Rome (Acts 25:11). According to Roman law the request had to be granted. Early in 61 Paul made the sea voyage to Rome as a prisoner (Acts 27–28). Paul thus set foot on the longed for soil of Rome early in 61, but as a prisoner.

When Paul wrote and came to Rome there already existed there a Church of very high repute among Christians (1:8). Direct accounts concerning the founders and the establishment of the Roman Church are lacking, but with regard to the beginning of the Church in Rome the following is possible or probable: there was in Rome a considerable number of Jews, estimated at perhaps 50,000. The Jews were also attracted by the importance of Rome and not least by the commerce of the city. Thirteen Roman synagogues are individually known from scattered accounts, and extended Jewish graves in the catacombs were recently rediscovered. Paul also contacted the Jewish community when he came to Rome but was rejected by it (Acts 28:17–28). According to Acts 2:10, however, there were also some Jews from Rome among those who had come to Jerusalem and witnessed there the first Christian Pentecost. When they witnessed the outpouring of the Holy Spirit and the other miracles, some of them may have become Christians. Returned to Rome they could have been the first messengers of the gospel here. Or perhaps others also came as its messengers to Rome by virtue of the urgency with which Rome attracted everything. Just as eastern religions had infiltrated Rome for centuries so now, at any rate, Christianity came there, basically because Rome was the center of the world. It was just as Tacitus (*Annals* 15:44) expressed it from his standpoint: "Everything detestable and shameless flows together in Rome and everything is celebrated." The growth of the community was meanwhile interrupted by a decree of the emperor Claudius who in 49 banished the Jews from Rome. If we correctly understand the accounts of Sueton (*Claudius* 25), the pagan historian, the reasons were quarrels and outbreaks of violence in the Jewish community because some acknowledged Jesus as the Messiah and other rejected him. Those Christians who had previously been Jews were also expelled, for these Jewish Christians were nothing but a Jewish sect as far as the Roman authorities were concerned. Only those Christians who had previously been Gentiles were allowed to remain. The Church in Rome was thus from then on a Gentile Christian Church. It probably remained Gentile Christian for the most part even though the emperor's extradition decree was lifted after a few years and the Jews could return. We see from the apostle Paul's Epistle to the Romans that the Gentile Christians are at that time in the majority. Paul addresses his readers and speaks of them as if they were all Gentile Christians (1:5f., 13–15; 11:13). Precisely in the Epistle to the Romans (9–11) Paul says, with deeply moving words, that so few out of Israel have become believers.

2 PAUL'S EPISTLE TO THE ROMANS

The Epistle to the Romans like all of Paul's epistles is a genuine letter, not a theological treatise. This letter is also a talk to people and a conversation with them. Naturally the epistle is no everyday letter. It was not written in an hour, as one wrote uncounted letters at that time, just as we do today. The epistle is too large in scope and too important in content for that.

The Epistle to the Romans is nevertheless not a personal letter, such as other Pauline epistles—to the Corinthians, to the Galatians, to the Philippians. Paul had personally founded and repeatedly visited the communities to which he wrote these latter epistles. He knew the condition and the concerns of these communities in detail and strove in his letters to lend them assistance in all matters. Not so in the Epistle to the Romans for Paul is not personally acquainted with the Roman community. He is not their very own apostle. For this reason he cannot and will not interfere with their affairs. He only wants to state his message or, as he announces in 2:16, his "gospel."

What for Paul according to this epistle is the nature of the gospel is for us today not only of great interest but also an authoritative norm. What is it then? It is first and foremost the message of Christ, the Son of David and the Son of God (1:3f; 9:5; 15:8). As the Mediator between God and the world he has atoned for sin and restored peace (3:25f; 5:1–21). As the Risen One he is the Lord of the Church and the world (10:6.9). One day the judgment of God will take place through him (2:16). To a large extent then Paul wants to speak in the Epistle to the Romans of the significance of the gospel for the salvation of the world and for the salvation of each individual. Paul understands this theme principally under the terms of justification of man before God, for he who can stand up before God as a righteous man will live (1:17). Yet first of all Paul has to show that man has never attained and can never attain justification by himself, that he thus was and is lost (1:18; 3:20). But now the justification which God gives to man must be proclaimed (3:21). Man is capable of grasping it in faith (3:21; 4:25). It is bestowed upon him in the sacrament (6:1–11). It is liberation from the law (7:1–25), and community of spirit in return (8:1–39). In Rom 9–11 Paul deals with the question of the salvation of Israel, which grieved him, in a detailed, appended excursus. As already in verses 6:12–23, in 12:1–15, 13 Paul deals conclusively with the fulfillment of the freely given justification in the moral life of the Christian.

Nowhere in the New Testament is the nature of God's sanctification and man's guilt and justification as profoundly stated as in the Epistle to the Romans. What Paul says is not, however, something devised and invented by him which he adds on to the gospel: Paul says only what the gospel of Jesus says. Naturally the apostle expresses this same gospel after the cross is planted, and Christ as the Risen One is the Lord of the Church. Christ, in the gospels, looks forward to Easter as something in the future; Paul and the apostles look back on it as something that has happened. Another contrast to the gospel is the fact that Paul does not speak with the divine simplicity and pro-

fundity of Christ the Teacher, but rather as a man, a
theologian wrestling with questions. And Paul does so as a
pupil of the Jewish rabbis, who were his teachers. He speaks
with formulas and conceptions as he has learned them and
they are often unfamiliar to us. For this reason we can
often not immediately or easily understand his epistles,
but must strive to do so. Besides, the epistles of the apostle
Paul required explanatory interpretation already at the time
of the New Testament (2 Pet 3:15f).

But nevertheless Paul's teaching on justification is the
same as the word of Jesus in the gospel. Lk 18:9–14 reports the parable of the Pharisee and the tax collector. The
Pharisee refers to his works: he imposes upon himself the
discipline of fasts and gives alms abundantly. The tax collector has nothing further to say than: may God have mercy
on me, a sinner. But Jesus says: "I assure you, this man
went down to his home acquitted of all guilt." Thus not
one's own work brings about justification before God but
rather it is given by the gift of God. In Mt 5:6 the Lord
says: "Blessed are those who hunger and thirst after holiness, for they will be fully satisfied." They will be filled
by God. Those who long for justification will receive it
as God's gift. Christ and Paul say that justification is not
the work of man but the gift of God. Paul's only addition
to the gospel is his statement that God now gives this
justification for the sake of Christ's work of salvation.

What Paul says is a timeless answer to the questions of
an either-or which always exist in the Church and which
must always be answered anew: law or spirit? narrowness
or freedom? limitation through tradition or creative re-

newal of faith? work of man or grace of God? achievement and reward or trust in God's gift?, ultimately: man or God? Paul has decided these questions in favor of the risk of freedom and of faith, in favor of the risk of the spirit and of grace. Paul does not make this decision out of his own human boldness—that would be impudence of man before God; rather, because these questions are thus answered by the words and deeds of Christ, and this answer is always set forth before the Church.

The schematic arrangement of the table of contents may simplify a survey of the contents of the Epistle to the Romans; see pages 5–7.

THE EPISTLE TO THE ROMANS

I INTRODUCTION

1: 1–17

At all times and among all peoples letters are written and all cultures develop thereby special forms and styles. We too have a specific form for our letters: date and salutation at the beginning, the main section with the expositions, and in conclusion the greetings. Antiquity also cultivated a letter form in which the oriental and Jewish form on the one hand and the Graeco-Roman on the other differed very little. In accordance with this style the name of the sender stands at the very beginning of the letter, to which the name of the recipient is joined with a word of greeting. Then often follows a word of thanks to God for good news which has come to the letterwriter. The letter then enters upon its subject matter. It is concluded by messages and greetings at the end.

1 SENDER AND RECIPIENTS OF THE EPISTLE

1: 1–7

1:1 Paul, servant of Christ Jesus, called to the apostolate and set apart to proclaim the Good News now made known by God,

2 as he had promised it of old through his prophets in Holy Writ,

3 the gospel of his Son, who as regards the flesh was born of the line of David,

4 but according to the spirit of holiness was constituted the mighty Son of God by his resurrection from the dead, Jesus Christ our Lord.

5 Through him we have received grace and the apostolic office, whose purpose is to bring men of all nations to honor his name by the submission of faith.

6 Among these nations you, who have been called to belong to Jesus Christ, are included.

7 To all Gods beloved, saints by vocation, at Rome, grace be to you and peace from God our Father and the Lord Jesus Christ.

With mention of the sender (1:1) and the recipients (1:7) and the offering of thanks (1:8), Paul follows the epistolary style of antiquity. But what is otherwise a short, formalized address Paul has often developed into a longer sentence, yet never to a greeting as full of meaning as here (1:1–7), a greeting without compare in the entire epistolary literature of antiquity. In an exhaustive addition to the name of the sender Paul introduces himself to the Roman Church, for until now he is unknown to her and must first of all gain a relationship to her. The fact that he is writing to a community not founded by him, whereby he is acting against his principles (15:20f; 2 Cor 10:15f), certainly requires justification and motivation. For this reason he sets forth in detail in the supplement to his name the extensive mission to the Gentiles which has fallen to him (1:5f), for it is in the execution of this mission that he writes and wishes to come to Rome.

(1:1) The first thing that Paul says about himself is that
he is the servant of Christ Jesus.[1] It does not go without saying that the pious man considers himself the servant of God
(or perhaps more correctly the slave of God). The Greek
has never considered his relationship to God in this way. He
believes that a free man may be no one's servant, not even
God's. "How could that man be happy who serves any one
at all" (Plato, Gorgias 491). Yet like the oriental, the godly
man of the Old and New Testaments states with that formula that he belongs to his God, simply and unconditionally. Accordingly the devout in the Old Testament often
call themselves the servants of God; in the Psalms those
who pray often refer to themselves in this way (26:9; 30:17;
88:51). But when it is the great fathers of the old covenant,
the friends of God like Abraham, Moses, Josuah and David
who are called the servants of Gods, then it is no longer a
term of lowliness but the highest title of honor. The
oriental knows of the honor of service to a noble master,
that is, of intimate association with him. Thus it is above
all an honor to stand in the service of God. If then the New
Testament, as in the parables of Jesus, often speaks of man
as the servant of God (Mt 24:45–51; 25:14–30; Lk 12:37;
17:7–10), it is not by any means the entire Christian understanding of man before God. The Christian is also son and
heir before God (Gal 4:6f; Rom 8:15f). And since he stands
in the service of God the Father and of Christ the Lord,
and thereby under their protection, he knows he is free
from all uncanny and demonic powers in the world (1 Cor
8:5). The servant of Christ is the free man of Christ, just
as the free man is the servant of Christ (1 Cor 7:22).

Yet Paul calls himself the servant of Christ not only in the general sense just explained, but also in the special sense, that as an apostle he stands in the service of Christ (as in Phil 1:1). Paul was added only later to the twelve apostles originally called by Christ (as "one born out of due time," Paul himself says in 1 Cor 15:8). For this reason his opponents disputed his full apostolic right (2 Cor 11–12). And against them Paul insists on his full apostleship. He has truly been summoned as an apostle. The call took place through the appearance of Christ to Paul, the persecutor of the Christians, before the gates of Damascus (Acts 9:1–30). Paul is thus no lesser apostle, but as one called directly by Christ he is an apostle authorized in a special way. (With the same deep conviction Paul speaks thereof in Gal 1:1, for precisely in the Epistle to the Galatians he must defend his ministry against his opponents.)

Paul emphasizes his true calling. He was singled out for the preaching of the gospel. When did this occur? In the summons before Damascus, or perhaps much earlier, as a selection from the very beginning according to the plan of God, as Paul says in Gal 1:15: "He set me apart even before my birth, and called me by his grace."

What was and what is, therefore, an apostle? He is not a master but a servant, called and ordered to come without being asked. He is an apostle, that is, a messenger, the messenger of another, and as such he is not to proclaim himself but precisely this other. He is singled out and separated from the community. He is alone and delivered up, he calls nothing his own but the word and the gift of God which he has to convey. Of course he brings God's gospel, thus the message of salvation from God. But just as God is much different than man imagines so also is his message different. It can be vexation as well as salvation. Its word can not be proved, it can only be believed. Belief certainly has its reasons but so does unbelief. The messenger of this word is therefore always questionable and unfamiliar in the world. The grandeur of his ministry is hidden. In truly moving passages Paul speaks repeatedly of the almost unbearable burden and grace of this charge. One must read all of these passages together: 1 Cor 4:9–13; 2 Cor 4:8–13; 6:3–10; 11:23–33.

(1:2) If the gospel as God's message is unexpected and strange to man it nevertheless does not come into the world as something entirely new. God has announced it in advance through the prophets, i.e. in the Old Testament. These testimonies are set down in the scriptures of the old covenant.[2] Just as in the entire New Testament Paul sees in the Old Testament a testimony for Christ, and the Church has always understood and interpreted the Old Testament in this way. The Church does not mean to say that the prophets knew clearly about the cross of Christ, and spoke about it in mysterious terms comprehensible only to themselves. Rather God proclaimed the testimony; but only now, after Christ and the cross of Christ have been revealed, is the previously hidden sense of the words of the Old Testament disclosed. Now it can be seen that everything is ordered on Christ as the hidden mid-point of time and flows toward him. He is the fulfillment of everything, God's great Yes to all promises and longings (2 Cor 1:20). This interpretation is thus no artificial insertion into Scripture, but the discovery and disclosure of its sense and of the course of salvation history from the Old Testament to the New. Announced in advance in the Holy Scriptures the gospel is not merely a thing of today, but has the dignity and verification of great age.

(1:3f) We read here an important testimony of what Paul believed and taught about Jesus Christ: Christ is the Son of God. To be sure Paul can say of man that he is the son and heir of God (Gal 4:6), but here, as elsewhere (8:3; 1 Cor 1:9; Gal 4:4), Paul grants Christ a completely unique and incomparable sonship. As this Son Christ abode with God in eternity before he appeared in the flesh as the Son of David, that is, before he became man, born of David's family. Israel awaits the Messiah as the royal offspring of David. Like the gospels (Mt 1:1; 9:27; Lk 1:32; Jn 7:42), the epistles of Paul teach that this expectation is now fulfilled, for Jesus the Son of David came as the Messiah. In his human life on earth the glory of the Son of God was hidden—hidden until the renunciation in death on the cross. But in his resurrection from the dead the divine sonship broke through once more and he was raised up to God. His divine abundance of power was revealed to the whole world and he was appointed Lord of the Church and the world in all divine majesty. (An ancient hymn, which Paul records in his Epistle to the Church in Philippi, Phil 2:5–11, declares the same teaching about Christ.) And this Christ is the substance of the gospel of God (1:1).

(1:5) Paul received the right and the duty to preach the gospel directly from this Lord of the Church. His task is

to bring about obedience of faith through this preaching.
Paul often uses this formulation, obedience of faith, which
makes clear what faith is. It occurs when the hearing of the
word is followed by obedience to it. Faith is not only a
matter of intelligence. It is not a mere belief in doctrines.
Nor is it merely an emotional impulse. It is submission,
yet a submission not only to the teaching Church but to
the God who speaks in revelation, and it is submission to
the reality of God in Christ. Among the apostles an agreement was reached—the New Testament mentions it repeatedly (Acts 15:12; Gal 2:7-9)—that the twelve first-
called apostles were to preach the gospel among the Jews,
Paul among the Gentiles. As apostle to the Gentiles Paul
has the right to write to the Church in Rome, which was
certainly made up for the most part, if not entirely, of
Gentiles.

(1:6) The Christian state of the Romans is described.
They are called from among the Gentiles. It is the call of
God, not merely the individual intention and desire to
convert, which constitutes the Christian. It is important
for the entire New Testament, for the gospels as well as
for Paul's epistles, to reiterate the fact that the first step
in becoming a Christian is God's grace. The Epistle to the
Romans (see under 9:16) will further emphasize that in
the whole work of salvation God is first and man second.
If this is a reason for modesty in the Christian, it is also a
reason for confidence. God takes the first step and always
begins anew. For this reason faith may be confident: "No
matter what our conscience may reproach us with, God is
greater than our conscience" (1 Jn 3:20).

(1:7) Just as they are called Christians so are they also God's beloved and his saints. All three titles mean the same thing in content. In his love, which preceded man from eternity, God has summoned the faithful and bestowed his gift upon them. Thus by vocation they are saints. What does this word mean? In the Bible of the Old and the New Testament God is called the Most Holy ("the Most Saint"),[3] whereby in Hebrew this word really means: he who is separated and isolated from the world. He is the "wholly Other." Thus the seraphim, hovering over God's throne and covering their faces and entire figures with their wings, call out to one another: " 'Holy, holy, holy is the Lord of hosts!' they cried one to the other. 'All the earth is filled with his glory' " (Is 6:1-4). God is the eternally Holy and whatever he calls into his realm, whatever he fills up with his presence, becomes holy: the holy angels, the Holy City Jerusalem (Mt 4:5), God's holy people and—in the New Testament—God's elect, his Church, who are called the saints (8:27; 12:13; 15:25). Thus if the Church is called holy this does not originally signify a special moral confirmation or a saintlike perfection in the following of God's commandment; the title signifies the summoning of the Church into God's community and dominion. This summoning naturally includes the separation from sin, since sin contradicts above all community with God. Yet here also the moral action of man follows out of the gift of God which preceded him. Man is capable of striving after a holy life because God has sanctified him. Paul must occasionally censure his congregations severely on account of their errors, but nevertheless he calls their members saints. The Church is always the Church of sinners, yet the holy Church of God. Accordingly all Christians are saints, not just a few who are especially perfect.

Paul's greeting wishes the Church grace and peace. Paul probably created this formula of salutation, which is then used repeatedly in the New Testament and ever since in the Church. No apostle has reflected as intensively or spoken as elucidatingly about the nature of grace as the loving, forgiving, newly creative turning of God toward man. Grace was an especially precious word to Paul and he therefore included it in his salutation. The word peace, however, is the centuries-old salutation of Israel, his people. The word does not signify merely a personal disposition of peace and quiet, but rather the state of reconciliation with God and thereby the rescue and salvation of man which, according to Paul, Christ brings as the gift of God. Paul therefore mentions them both as mediators of grace and peace.

The beneficent God is called our Father. The history of religion is aware that other religions, not merely the New Testament and the Christian faith, are also able to call God the Father. Jewish prayer salutations of later times also sporadically call God the Father. But nowhere is God called our Father with such certainty and sincerity as in the New Testament. This term expresses the unique certainty with which the disciples of Jesus, according to his gospel, were able to believe in and experience God as a loving Father. Even the history of religion recognizes, therefore, in the name of God the Father the clear and pure expression of the belief of the disciples of Christ, and in the prayer Our Father the distinguishing mark and the constitutional charter of the Church of Jesus Christ.

2 REASON, INTENTION AND THEME OF THE EPISTLE

1:8–17

1: 8 First I give thanks to my God through Jesus Christ for all of you, because your faith is proclaimed all over the world.

9 Indeed God, whom I serve in all sincerity by proclaiming the Good News about his Son, is my witness how unceasingly I make mention of you,

10 always imploring at my prayers that somehow by God's will I may at last come to you after a safe journey.

11 I really long to see you that I may impart some spiritual gift to you to strengthen you,

12 or rather, that among you I may be comforted together with you by that faith which is common to us both, yours and mine.

13 Brothers, I would not have you unaware that I have often proposed to come to visit you, that I may gather some fruit among you also as well as among the rest of the Gentiles, but I have been prevented until now.

14 To Greeks and to barbarians, to wise and unwise, I owe a debt,

15 so that for my part I am eager to preach the Good News to you also who are at Rome.

16 I am certainly not ashamed of the Good News, for it is the power of God to bring about salvation for everyone that has faith, for Jew first and then Greek.

17 For in it God's way of sanctifying from faith unto faith is revealed. As it is written,

"The holy man lives by faith."

Paul tries first of all to create a personal relationship between himself and the recipients of the epistle. He
describes his previous relation to the Church in Rome.
Until now he was able to think of her only from afar, and
he did so honestly and sincerely. For a long while, however,
he has wished to come to Rome, whose Church he esteems
so highly. He has been prevented so far by compelling circumstances. Now he hopes soon to sojourn in Rome to
preach the gospel there and, still more, to be comforted
and strengthened there.

(1:8) Following the epistolary usage of his time[4] Paul
begins with thanks to God whom, with an expression of
deep feeling of the nearness and the love of God, he calls
his God. Paul gives thanks that people throughout the
world know of the rise of a Christian congregation in Rome.
A Church in Rome means that the great and proud capital
of the world acknowledges the cross of the Lord. A Church
in Rome—what that must have meant for the progress of
the mission! Rome is the middle of the world and whoever
possesses its middle possesses it completely. Paul praises
the faith of the Roman Church. Will we not, as Catholic
Christians, read advisedly that the faith of that Church, in
which the teaching function of the Church resides in a
special way since that time, is praised in a special way from
the very beginning? This Church has this honor from the
very beginning.

(1:9f) Paul does not think of the Roman Church only
now, on the occasion of his epistle, but is continually mind-
ful of her. It is so important for Paul to affirm this fact that
he calls upon God as his witness. He before whom the heart

of man is open knows Paul's prayers for the Church in Rome. Service to the gospel is for Paul a priestly office. Paul is not merely a preacher in his congregation but a priest, the mediator between God and the world (15:16). Paul performs his apostolic service to the gospel not only by untiring external activity, by journeys, sermons, epistles and admonitions, but also in the innermost spirit, by the conversing of his heart with God and the priestly intercession for the congregation. The intention of his prayers again and again becomes a request that his path may be led safely, by God's will, to Rome. Here as always Paul considers his missionary paths and those of his coworkers determined by the will of God (1 Cor 4:19; 16:7, 12).

(1:11) What does Paul want in Rome? He wants to bestow the Spirit's gift of grace, perhaps in the words of his sermon, in the comfort of encouragement, in the strengthening testimony of faith and certainly in the ceremony of worship (Acts 20:7). Paul would surely be able to say of any Christian that he mediates the Spirit's gift of grace, but the apostle can do so in a special and universally valid way, as Paul says in 2 Cor 1:15: when he comes to Corinth for the second time, the Christians there will enjoy "a second opportunity for grace." Paul is not only a preacher but also a priestly mediator (1:9).

(1:12) Paul corrects himself immediately with polite tact. On a visit in Rome he would not only bestow but also receive. He wants to be comforted in and with the community of faith. He is not the rich man who has only to give; or the teacher who alone speaks while all others listen; or the prince of the Church who imparts grace. To be sure he considers himself the bearer of the apostolic office in which the Church is founded and endures. But he does not suppose that the Church and the world exist through the labor that he performs, not to mention the activity which he carries on. He is a brother who desires comfort from his fellows. He is the poor man who is enriched by their faith. He has never shied away from speaking, as a human being, of his poverty before the community. He himself says that he made his way to Corinth in great inner distress, concerned whether the metropolis, extremely rich in intellect and money, would listen to the gospel: "It was in weakness and fear and much trepidation that I presented myself to you" (1 Cor 2:3).

And his biographer, Luke, reports that when Paul was on the way to Rome the Roman Christians came out as far as the Three Taverns to meet him. "On seeing them Paul gave thanks to God and took courage" (Acts 28:15). Even a man like Paul was in need of kindness. A man like Paul, who as a minister and witness to the faith had a voice in laying the foundation of the history of the west, considered himself a brother among brothers, a man among men. That is certainly a part of his human and spiritual greatness.

(1:13) Paul mentions a still further purpose of his Roman voyage: he wants to gather fruit and bring in the harvest. He wants to win new believers through his missionary preaching, just as he has done everywhere among the Gentiles, for he has been charged with the mission among the Gentiles (1:5). Paul calls the Christians brothers, just as in the entire New Testament the Christians consider and call one another brothers and sisters. The New Testament thereby takes up the linguistic usage of the Jewish nation which by virtue of the blood unity of its ancestors felt itself to be a great family. Jesus took over the expression for his band of disciples. He calls his disciples his brothers and sisters (Mk 3:35), and the disciples are a great brotherhood (Mt 23:8). But this Christian brotherhood is no longer the merely natural community of blood, as before. It is something new and different because it is formed around Christ as the new center and the heavenly Father is the one Father to all (Mt 12:50): "Anyone that does the will of my Father in heaven is brother or sister or mother to me." The name and salutation of brother and sister disappeared from the everyday life of the Church, but was maintained in the monastic families. It is also still permitted to those outside the monastery to address members of the monastic family as brother and sister, an address which is not self-evident to a stranger. When we also call lay nurses "sisters"[5] a fact known to history comes to light: that worldly humanity is a daughter of Christian caritas, even if the daughter often no longer knows her mother.

(1:14f) It is not only Paul's longing to come to Rome, however: it is his duty and obligation. He owes the gospel to all men, to Greeks and barbarians,[6] to learned and unlearned. In obedience to his commission Paul would thus like to preach the gospel also in Rome.

(1:16) Since Paul mentions the metropolis of Rome, concern about his intention and duty to preach the gospel there already oppresses him. Will the message find open ears and willing hearts in the capital and center of the mighty empire, and in the city of high intellectual culture?

Paul sees this real world and stands firm against it for he is not ashamed of the gospel. He knows that it is not weakness but strength—God's strength, of course, and only his. For this reason it need not and must not be willing to borrow aid and support elsewhere (from the society or the state, for example). That would be to mistrust its true strength. In the gospel God's undefiled strength is at work. For this reason it is a powerful, living, active force. And this strength works salvation. Salvation has been an important term of religions for centuries and is especially so in this very age. The Old Testament hope, like the religion of the pagan world, awaits more and more urgently the Redeemer who will bring salvation to the lost world. In Rome as elsewhere people were ready to honor as saviors[7] the emperors and kings who brought or were supposed to bring men peace, or wise men and teachers who brought the world light. To this world Paul must preach the true salvation and the true Savior: faith will find him. The Epistle to the Romans itself will present in detail how salvation comes to faith. The Christ is salvation for all, that is (in contrast to 1:14), for both Jew and Greek. From the point of view of salvation history humanity falls into these two divisions. Some are Jews who serve God according to the written law, and the others the Gentiles who are to search for him according to the natural law innate in them (2:14). Should the Jews suppose that they could earn it through their own works they would be in error (3:28–30). Paul mentions the Jews first because he acknowledges their precedence as the chosen people (9:4f). For this reason in every city of all his journeys between Jerusalem and Rome—as we are

often told in the Acts of the Apostles—Paul always goes
first of all into the synagogue to preach. Only when he is
rejected there does he go to the Gentiles.

(1:17) Salvation is the gospel since it brings God's
justification. Paul is a son of Israel, which for centuries has
borne the hardship of the fulfillment of the law and has
often defended the law, in the immediately preceding
centuries, at the cost of belongings and blood—all this in
order to obtain justification before God. And Paul would
say that all these pains were taken with reason. To be just
in God's eyes or to live unjustly under his anger is certainly a question of life and death, for the just man will be
welcomed and saved by his God whereas the unjust man
is lost. And Paul might well say that whoever does not
understand this has a dull and obtuse mind. If the gospel
now brings justification it also brings salvation.

But how does this come about? One of the main intentions of the Epistle to the Romans is to answer this
question. Paul's concept of justification has, thereby, a
peculiar double meaning. Justification is both that justice
which belongs to God as the supreme Lord and by virtue
of which he rules the world justly, as well as that justification that God gives to man and with which he makes man
just, or "justified" (3:26). If God is just he is just in a different way than man. Even as God's beauty creates the
beauty of the world, and his life all the life in the world, so
all his attributes overflow abundantly into his world. All
of his attributes are creative. So God is also just while he
makes man just; thus his justice is also his grace; and the

judgment he exercises is also the salvation he works. Paul
sees this nature and action of God revealed in the gospel.
It reveals God's justice in that atonement for sin is demanded in the cross, and God's salvation in that the cross
produces salvation for the faithful. "For our sakes God
made sin of him who knew no sin, so that in him we might
become God's holiness" (2 Cor 5:21). But it is faith which
apprehends this salvation.

Paul summarizes everything with a saying from the
prophet Habacuc: "The holy man lives by faith." Paul
wants to say that in the distant past—when Israel still
toiled under the law—God promised that one day, in the
time of salvation, he would save not for the sake of the
works which man supposes he can produce but only for
the sake of the faith which grasps the cross of Christ. Although Habacuc himself may not have comprehended his
saying so clearly modern Old Testament exegesis is convinced that Paul, in his interpretation of the prophet's
saying, understood altogether correctly the meaning and
tendencies of the Old Testament, inasmuch as the Old
Testament in its development through the centuries points
more and more away from the works of man and toward the
grace of God.[8]

In further sections of the Epistle to the Romans Paul
will further unfold the theme of the santification of God
and of man. He makes clear why the sanctification of the
crucified Christ can be the sanctification of us all (5:1–21),
and then explains the question of how the believer ever
personally obtains the sanctification of Christ for himself

in the act of faith (3:21; 4:25) and in the fulfillment of the
sacraments (6:1–14). Paul shows how sin was operative in
the time of the law of the old covenant (7:1–25), and how,
in the new covenant, sanctification now becomes a reality
in the Spirit (8:1–39).

FOOTNOTES TO CHAPTER I

¹ In this sequence of the two words, Christ Jesus, Christ (Messiah) is still a functional name and not a personal name, as in the closely following titular, Jesus Christ. The title Christ in 1:1 still contains the original apostolic confession: This Jesus is the awaited Messiah=Christ.

² The history of the Church testifies again and again to the fact that the Old Testament is not merely a testimony for the New, but that the New Testament, precisely because of its tie to the Old, can be unfamiliar and can become an annoyance.

³ [In English usage, the term "saint" (from Latin sanctus, "holy") has a very special and limited application, as a noun, and is otherwise rendered by its adjectival equivalent, "holy."—tr]

⁴ For example: in a letter of the second century A.D. recently come to light from the sands of Egypt, the sailor Apion, referring to a stormy passage, begins his letter to his father: "I give thanks to my Lord, Serapis (i.e. his God), that he rescued me."

⁵ [The German word for nurse is *Schwester*, "sister."—tr]

⁶ The usual distinction in antiquity between Greeks and non-Greeks is made originally according to language. All those who do not speak Greek are barbarians (i.e. those who speak unintelligibly). Yet the Romans themselves do not speak Greek. Are they thus barbarians, in Paul's opinion? Certainly not. The Romans also belong to the world of Greek culture which had long since become the Graeco-Roman world. The Romans, to whom Paul is writing an epistle in Greek, are thus identified according to culture and intellect as "Greeks."

⁷ Emperors like Nero and Hadrian are called "Savior of the World" in inscriptions like Christ in Jn 4:42; philosophers are honored as saviors in the writings of their disciples.

[8] The formula "from faith unto faith" is obscure. Does it mean that sanctification begins as faith, remains faith and ends as faith, and thus is never earned by works but always received in faith as God's gift? The formula would then emphasize the purity of faith. This is a possible interpretation.

II Sin and Perdition of Men

1:18—3:20

Not out of his own work and merit but only out of God's gift is man capable of being just. Paul wants to demonstrate this in the Epistle to the Romans. He shows first of all what man was and is capable of on his own: only wrongdoing, which must place him under the anger of God. Without God's freely given sanctification the world would have gone irretrievably to its ruin under the anger and judgment of God. Paul proves this for the two divisions of mankind, for the Gentiles (1:18–32) and for the Jews (2:1; 3:20), thus for everyone without exception.

1 THE OFFENSE OF THE GENTILES

1:18–32

1:18 The wrath of God is being revealed from heaven against all ungodliness and wickedness of those men who in wickedness stifle the truth of God.
19 Here is the reason: what may be known about God is manifest to them, because God has manifested it to them.
20 Since the creation of the world his invisible attributes are clearly seen—especially his everlasting power and divinity, which are understood through the things that are made. And so they are without excuse,

21 because although they knew God, they did not glorify him
as God or give thanks, but their reasonings became absurd,
and their senseless minds were darkened.

22 While professing to be wise, they became fools,

23 and they exchanged the glory of the incorruptible God for
an image made like corruptible man and to birds and
four-footed beasts and creeping things.

24 Therefore God has given them up, in the lustful desires
of their heart, to uncleanness, so that they dishonor their
own bodies—

25 they who exchanged the truth of God for a lie and wor-
shipped and served the creature rather than the Creator
who is blessed forever, amen.

26 For this cause God has given them up to shameful lusts;
for their women have exchanged natural intercourse for
what is against nature,

27 and in the same way men too, having given up natural
intercourse with women, have burned in their lusts toward
one another, men with men practicing that well-known
shamelessness and receiving in their own persons the fitting punishment of their perversity.

28 And as they resolved against having a good knowledge of
God, God has given them up to a seared conscience so
that they do what is morally disgraceful.

29 They are steeped in dishonesty, wickedness, greed, ill-will;
they are overflowing with envy, murderous intent, strife,
deceit, rancor; they secretly spread false reports; they
openly calumnate, they hate God, they are insulting.

30 They are proud, vain, boastful, ingenious in evil, disobedient to parents.

31 They lack conscience, constancy, love, pity.

32 Although they are aware of the decree of God that those
who do such things are worthy of death, they not only do
them, but applaud others who do them.

Paul turns first to the Gentiles. In his missionary preaching he may have often reproached them with their lapses,

disclosed the punishment already being executed, and announced that still to come, just as he does in 1:18–32.

(1:18f) God has revealed himself also to the Gentiles: they could and did recognize him. But they suppressed recognition and truth with force. Their idolatry is thus no unknowing innocence or unfortunate development of the culture but disobedience and wrongdoing, and the worship of many gods is blameworthy impiety. God must answer it with his anger.

(1:20f) God has marked creation with his traces. "The heavens declare the glory of God" (Ps 18:2–7). For that reason the invisible God is recognizable to the creatures in creation, insofar as reason can conclude upon reflection that there is a God (only this, of course; man cannot know the entire mysterious nature of God with reason alone; nor God as the Father, whom Jesus Christ has revealed). Paul expresses the same conviction on the Areopagus in Athens (Acts 17:27f): "God is not far from anyone of us. For in him we live and move and have our being." And likewise John says (1:10): the Light and the Word of God was always in the world. But the world did not recognize him. Men were not lacking in perception but certainly in the willingness to act upon it. Man should have acknowledged God with honor and gratitude as the Creator and the Giver of all good things. But he refused to do so in order not to have to acknowledge his dependence as a creature. For this reason man is unpardonable.

(1:21b–23) Punishment follows the offense. Man must stand either under the glory of God or the nothingness of idols.

(1:24-28) The punishment takes place in that God gives men free reins into and within their sins. He punishes man for sin by abandoning him hopelessly to sin. Paul begins his portrayal of the moral disintegration, with which God punishes impiety, three times with an ominous: "God has given them up to sin" (1:24,26,28). The punishment corresponds to the offense. Impiety is the reversal of the creator with the creature, of truth with lies. From this fundamental perversion follows the overturning of every order of creation in the unnatural use of other creatures. Man first dishonors God. Then he dishonors himself. So God gave them up to unchastity, with which they disgraced themselves (1:24f). He gave them up to still deeper aberration and the especially dishonorable passion of unnatural fornication (1:26f). God gave up those who were not willing to know and acknowledge him to absurdity and all manner of disgrace (1:28).

(1:29-32) Paul describes finally the complete dissolution of the moral order with a long list of all possible sins and vices. Such catalogs are found in other biblical and non-biblical texts of that time, with which philosophical or religious ethics wishes to hold a mirror up to the age (thus also Wis 14:22-31; further catalogs in the writings of Paul himself, such as 1 Cor 6:9; Gal 5:19-21; Eph 5:3f among others).[1] Paul's list reveals the biblical, New Testament impact, at any rate where he denounces the lack of love and pity (1:31). This is an echo of the Christian commandment of love. Such words are hardly to be found in pagan catalogs of vice.

Paul's judgment on heathendom, the world of Graeco-

Roman culture in which he lived, is extraordinarily gloomy and severe. Did he see nothing of its beauty and grandeur which are still wondrous to us today in its ruins? Is its wisdom only folly to Paul, its splendor only darkness, its grandeur only perversity? Only the Roman state can he perhaps judge more favorably (13:1–7). Paul speaks as a prophet who measures everything according to his highest and eternally worthy God and the service of God in faith and life. Against that everything else becomes worthless and unimportant.

2 THE JUDGMENT OF GOD

2: 1–16

2: 1 And so you are inexcusable, O man, whoever you are who judge. Your judgment passed on another is your own condemnation.

2 For you, who sit in judgment, yourself commit the same sins. We know that the condemnation of God is in accord with the truth and is leveled against those who are guilty of such sins.

3 Do you think, O man, who judge those who do such things and do the same yourself, that you will escape the condemnation of God?

4 Or do you despise the wealth of his goodness, patience, and long-suffering? Do you not know that the goodness of God is meant to lead you to repentance?

5 But according to your obstinacy and unrepentant heart, you treasure up to yourself wrath on the day of wrath, when the just judging of God,

6 who "will render to everyone according to his deeds" (Ps 61:13) will be revealed.

7 Life eternal he will give to those who by persevering in
good deeds seek glory, honor, and immortality;

8 but wrath and indignation will he visit on those that are
contumacious, that is to say, who refuse to submit to the
truth, but assent to iniquity.

9 Tribulation and anguish shall be the lot of every man who
is bent on evil-doing: of the Jew first and then of the
Greek;

10 but glory, honor, and peace will be the lot of every man
intent on doing good: of the Jew first and then of the
Greek,

11 since with God there is no favoritism.

12 Whoever have sinned, not having the Law, will perish
without respect to the Law, and whoever were bound by
the Law and have sinned will be judged by the Law.

13 Really it is not they who hear the Law that are holy in the
sight of God, but it is they who follow the Law that will
be sanctified.

14 When the Gentiles who have no law follow the dictates
of reason, and do what the Law prescribes, these, though
they have no law, are a law to themselves.

15 They show that the requirements of the Law are written
in their hearts. Their conscience bears the same testimony,
as also their thoughts, which alternately accuse or defend
them.

16 This will be evident on the day when God will judge the
secrets of men by Jesus Christ according to the gospel I
preach.

After Paul has preached the offense and punishment to
the Gentile, the Jew comes into Paul's and the reader's
view. As he who would like to rest on his possession of the
law, the Jew is addressed first in veiled language (2:1–16),
then openly (2:17–29).

(2:1–3) The Jew considered himself free from the
horrors and aberrations portrayed. But if he wanted to set

himself up as a judge over the others he would also condemn himself, for he also stands in contradiction to God
and therefore under God's judgment and anger. Judgment
is a dangerous weapon which strikes him who administers it
self-righteously (Mt 7:1–5). It would be a wicked error if
someone thought, while he condemned others, that he had
renounced sin and would escape the judgment of God.
One's conduct alone is decisive.

(2:4f) It would be another error if someone believed that
the judgment would not come at all simply because it
delays coming. God's patience and long-suffering are certain. But let man beware of no longer taking God seriously
for that reason. Rather God's goodness wants to leave time
for, and lead to repentance. A hard and impenitent heart
gathers anger above its head for the day of judgment.

(2:6–9a) Paul makes his own warning even more urgent
by means of a biblical saying which he quotes from Ps
61:13. For Paul as for his audience the word of God is
always the highest admonishing authority (2:6). Paul now
explains and applies the saying. God will reward each and
every man according to his works, says the Psalm. This contains two possibilities. Those who constantly strive to do
good and aspire to honor and glory will receive eternal life
(2:7). Those however who prefer wrongdoing to truth will
experience the anger and fury of God (2:8). The apostle
admonishes in utmost earnest. In order not to be ignored
he repeats both promise and threat (2:9,10).

(2:9b–11) Once again, as already in 1:16, appears the
order: first Jew, then Greek. The precedence of Israel in
salvation history applies both in good and in evil. To elec-

tion corresponds a greater responsibility. Israel's sin and punishment are therefore sooner and more severe because her knowledge and the favor she received were greater. The precedence of the Jew also applies, however, when the reward is to be received. Since the call of God goes out first to the Jew before the Gentile, he also receives the reward first (2:10). But nevertheless the priority does not concern the size of the reward. There is no favoritism with God. He never asks about the person, only about the deed.

(2:12f) The judgment is just and the same for Jews and Gentiles. Nonetheless the same judgment is only possible under the same law. Only the Jews have the written law, and not the Gentiles. For this reason the Jews are judged according to how they keep the law.

(2:14f) To be sure the Gentiles do not have the written law of Moses. But they know and have that law which is given to every man by his very nature. The Gentiles also, by the moral action of which they are capable and which they accomplish, prove that they know the law. Paul names two spheres in which man becomes conscious of the law: in the command of the heart and in the voice of the conscience.[2] Paul describes dramatically what takes place here: in the conscience—before and after the deed—thoughts stand embattled with one another. In thinking over a plan or a deed the thoughts of a man accuse one another and condemn or acquit the perpetrator. The inner hither-and-thither of accusation and defense takes place in the conscience of man, and man cannot withdraw from it. He feels himself bound, as to a law. It is not laid down in written form before him like the law of Moses before the Jews. But it is inscribed into his very nature.

(2:16) Jews and Gentiles will thus be judged according to the law. In the brightness of the last judgment, when the hidden secrets of men come to light, everything will thus finally be revealed. The judgment of God will be held off by Christ, the Judge of the world (cf. under 5:9). And Paul says that this is always his teaching, that this is his unchanging gospel. He seems to emphasize that the announcement of the judgment is gospel, i.e. the message of salvation.

Paul establishes unequivocally that God will judge according to one's works. "Really it is not they who hear the Law that are holy in the sight of God, but it is they who follow that Law that will be sanctified" (2:13). Likewise, for example, he says in 2 Cor 5:10: "We must all be laid open to inspection before the tribunal of Christ, each to receive his due in keeping with the good or evil he has done while he was in the body." Yet Paul also says (1:17): "The holy man lives by faith;" and (3:24): "We are sanctified by the gift of God;" and (3:28): "We hold that a man is sanctified by faith independently of the deeds prescribed by the Law."

Does Paul's teaching thus shatter into two fragments? Is there a "by-works-alone" and a "by-faith-alone?" A religion of law and a religion of grace? We may not charge Paul with having taught such incompatible things without having become aware of it. According to Paul God's gift alone, which faith apprehends, justifies. Man's works are not capable of justifying him before God. But the obedience of faith in which one submits oneself to God is also an obedience to action. Mere lip-service is never faith; rather as Paul himself says in Gal 5:6: "What counts is faith that expresses itself in love." Faith alone makes man holy but this faith, if it is otherwise genuine, is never alone but is always fulfilled in action. Therefore Paul can further state that the gospel does not abolish the demand of the law but for the first time demands aright and fulfills completely (3:31; 8:4), inasmuch as its claim is faith (4:3) and love (13:10). And the gospel does not rob the concept of God of its force by abolishing the judgment for the act of faith is still demanded in the judgment. It also remains true, of course, that the justification, through which alone man can stand steadfast before God, is never earned by him but is always given to him. Are these still, in the end, anti-theses which cannot be balanced? Then it remains in God's mystery and fullness of power how the gift of his justification to man is related to the word of judgment, which demands the fulfillment of the law by man. He has possibilities which we men neither have nor know. Every human form of thought must of course fall short and fail before the reality of God.

3 THE OFFENSE OF THE JEWS

2:17–29

2:17 Now you are called "Jew," and you rely on the Law. You glory in God,
18 you know his will; you approve the higher ideals, since you are informed by the Law.

19 You are confident that you are a guide to the blind, a light to those who are in darkness,

20 an instructor of the unwise, a teacher of children, since you have in the Law the pattern of knowledge and of truth.

21 You, therefore, who teach others, do you not teach yourself? You who preach against stealing, do you steal?

22 You who say that men should not commit adultery, do you commit adultery? You who abominate idols, do you plunder temples?

23 You who glory in the Law, do you dishonor God by transgressing the Law?

24 "The name of God," as it is written, "is maligned because of you among the Gentiles" (Is 52:5).

25 Circumcision is certainly useful if you keep the Law, but if you are a transgressor of the Law, your circumcision is the same as no circumcision.

26 If, then, the uncircumcised person keeps the precepts of the Law, will not his uncircumcision be counted as circumcision?

27 And he who is physically uncircumcised, provided he fulfills the Law, will condemn you who have a written Law and circumcision, and yet transgress the Law.

28 For he is not really a Jew who is so outwardly, nor is that man circumcised who is so outwardly, in the flesh.

29 But he is a Jew who is so inwardly, and real circumcision is a matter of the heart—something based on the spirit, not just on the letter of the Law. The praise of such a man comes not from men but from God.

The sermon of conversion turns in 2:17–19 in unveiled and urgent terms to the Jews, as Paul denounces Israel on account of the disproportion between the responsibility proceeding from her election and the conduct of her life.

(2:17) Paul admits to the Jew that he has been given a great deal. His pride has its reason. He has a name full of honor. A further claim to glory is the law, by virtue of which Israel has been since ancient times the people of order, of government, of culture and of religion, while other peoples were still without education and order, or lack them even today. God is Israel's God of the covenant who turned his election and love toward Israel.

(2:18) Israel knows the will of God by means of the law. The Jew knows what is important and decisive, while the Gentiles in their ignorance have fallen to all vices (1:18–32).

(2:19f) The Jew therefore regards himself as a guide of the blind and a light of the peoples. The self-assurance of the Jewish people is also expressed in Mt 15:14; 23:16, 24. The Jew is convinced that he has a missionary errand in the world. He regards the law as the incarnation of all knowledge and truth.

(2:21f) But what a contradiction and disproportion between pretension and reality! The Jew wants to convert the world and forgets to teach himself. He thinks he knows the subtle details of the moral law and he himself fails in the crudest and most elementary matters. Paul charges the Jews with theft, adultery, the plundering of temples.

(2:23) Through the discord between theory and practice the Jew dishonors not only the law, on which he so prides himself, but also God as the lawgiver.

(2:24) If the Jew is contemptible in the world the Jews' God of the covenant will also be slandered by the Gentiles. A prophet's saying (Is 52:5) confirms that this was already so throughout Israel's history.

(2:25) As on the law the Jew prides himself on his circumcision as the sign of the covenant which makes every Jew sure of his God and marks him as the property of his God. According to Jewish belief Abraham sits at the gate of hell and lets no one circumcised fall in. Paul warns the Jews not to deceive themselves with such hopes. Circumcision is the sign of the covenant. But it only has value, Paul warns, if you yourself keep the covenant by fulfilling the law. Otherwise circumcision is worthless or, drastically stated, it no longer exists.

(2:26) Paul dares draw the conclusion, scarcely bearable to a Jew: if an uncircumcised Gentile fulfills the demands of the law, then in the eyes of God he bears the honorary mark of circumcision.

(2:27) Gentiles who in fact fulfill the law bear witness against the Jewish people, who with written law and circumcision break the law. Paul checks any possible pride of the Jews that would like to rest on the possession of the law, disregard one's own sin and despise other peoples. The apostle's assertion that the Gentile will judge the Jew agrees with the saying of the Lord, Mt 12:41: "Ninevites will rise at the Judgment together with this nation and put it in the wrong, for on the preaching of Jonas they changed their evil ways."

(2:28f) Circumcision is not, when properly understood, something external and it is not to be accomplished on the flesh but on the heart. It is to take away the impurity of the heart. Its sense is a hidden, spiritual reality, like the joyous submission to God which is to be accomplished in the spirit. Only God knows this inner reality of man. He knows where true Jewry is, which merits his honor. He alone knows his true people, Israel, and he knows where this his people is, both within and beyond the limits of the Israel reckoned according to blood ancestry.

These sentences of the apostle must have been severe propositions for the Jews of his time. But Paul takes up thoughts of Old Testament prophecy which also warned the Jews not to trust self-righteously in the law and circumcision; thus Jer 4:4: "For the sake of the Lord be circumcised, remove the foreskins of your hearts, O men of Judea and citizens of Jerusalem, lest my anger break out like fire." Yet from Paul's times there are various sayings of serious Jewish teachers who saw the antithesis between the teaching and life in Israel, and who warned against false confidence. The Church Fathers' exegeses to Paul's words have explained, however, that they apply not only to Jewry but to every false, self-righteous church. Thus Origen, in his exegesis of the Epistle to the Romans (Migne, *Patrologia Graeca* 14:897), says that Paul's words concern not only the Jews but still more all those "who have only the name of religion and piety, but who lack the works of wisdom and faith, indeed, in greater earnest than others, us ourselves."

4 COVENANT AND FIDELITY

3:1–8

3:1 What advantage, then, remains to the Jew, or what is the use of circumcision?

2 Much, in every respect. First, the Jews had the oracles of God entrusted to them.

3 What then? If some of them have not been faithful, will their unfaithfulness nullify the faithfulness of God?

4 That must never be! God must prove true, even if all men are liars (Ps 115:11), as it is written,

"That you may be vindicated as just in your deeds,
  And may win your case when you are judged" (Ps 50:6).
5 But if our wickedness shows forth the justice of God, what
  shall we say? Is God unjust when he inflicts punishment?
  (I am speaking according to human standards.)
6 That must never be! Otherwise, how is God to judge the
  world?
7 But if by means of my fickleness the fidelity of God to his
  promises has been more abundantly proved to his glory,
  why am I still judged a sinner?
8 And why should we not do evil that good may come of it,
  as some calumniously accuse us of teaching. The condemnation of such is well deserved.

Paul has severely accused Israel. In 3:1–8 he permits an
objection of Jewry, which wants to defend itself.

(3:1) If the circumcision of the heart is the only true
and valid circumcision, then what does it mean to belong
to the historic Jewish chosen people? Has God not sealed
his covenant forever with the Jews? Does the covenant still
exist? What value is it still to have? One can in fact ask
such questions. Paul allows a listener to speak, who then
asks him this question. And the apostle answers that Israel's
advantages remain, yet there is no favoritism in the judgment. Paul is a Jew with the very proud conviction of a
Jew—that he belongs to the chosen people of God. As a
Jew he cannot let Israel have her dignity taken away. And
as a theologian he cannot admit that the advantages of
Israel have fallen away. God has given Israel his word of
love in the election. God's word must certainly always endure. If it does not hold good here, it does not hold good
anywhere. In Rom 9–11 Paul, passionately bound to his
people, returns once more to this question and discusses it.

(3:2) Paul begins to enumerate Israel's advantages. He

mentions as the first and most important advantage the fact
that to her were entrusted the words and revelations of
God, that is, both the law and the messianic promises.
(Diverted by other considerations the apostle does not mention any further advantages. In 9:2–5 others are enumerated.)

(3:3) Paul makes for himself and listens to another in-
terrogative objection. God was and is faithful. Will he
remain the Faithful One even when men were found to be
unbelieving and unfaithful? Paul hints at Israel and all her
unbelief and backsliding, from the worship of the golden
calf to the present rejection of the Messiah, Jesus. If, then,
Israel did not fulfill the duty of the covenant, will God
nevertheless keep the faith of the covenant?

(3:4) Paul emphatically rejects all doubts about God's
fidelity. God is true. His word, once given, remains forever.
God is the solely True One in face of man, deceitful without exception. Paul finds this stated in Ps 50:6. If man
wanted to suspect God's truthfulness and fidelity, if man
wanted to dare challenge God to a juridical investigation,
then God would always be in the right, and in a trial he
would remain forever the winner. Man, on the other hand,
would always stand unmasked as a liar.

Like the passage 2:25–29, the verses 3:1–8 may be said
not only to Israel but also to the Church. Israel has the law
and the promises as God's gift. The gift of God remains
even if Israel disregards it. The gospel and the sacraments
are given to the Church. They remain the word and the
effective signs, no matter how unworthy the dispensing
Church, no matter how inadequate the preaching may be,
no matter how indifferently the liturgy may be celebrated.

The fidelity of God is greater than all the infidelity of men.

(3:5) Paul replies to new objections that one can make. From what he has said thus far, one could conclude: the more unfaithful man is the greater the faithfulness of God, as his partner, proves to be. Thus there is certainly need of sin as a dark background, so that God's fidelity and justice can become all the more evident. If human sin thus serves the glorification of God, if sin is thus necessary in the plan of history, in order to finally reveal God's grandeur, is God not unjust if he uses the sin of man and nevertheless judges sin and condemns the sinner? That God is unjust is naturally a conclusion which Paul himself is terrified to contemplate. He excuses himself that he dares draw, by human means and logic, such a blasphemous conclusion.

(3:6) The apostle does not really enter into a conversation with the questioner and he does not bother unravelling his conclusions. He reminds the objector of what is also certain for him, that God is, after all, the Judge of the world. There may be unjust judges among men but this is surely impossible with God. Thus the conclusion that God could be unjust is impossible. The apostle will show further on (3:8) that such resourceful conclusions vis-à-vis God are only nonsense, indeed slander.

(3:7f) Yet Paul wrestles still further with the harassing question of human understanding. The falsehood of man only brings God's truth to light. By what right, then, is man condemned as a sinner? And Paul does not just imagine this objection but must actually listen to it. Some say of him that the logic of his teaching is: let us do evil, that

good may come of it! In Rom 6 (6:1ff) Paul speaks repeatedly of this insinuation made against him. There he
demonstrates that it is completely incorrect to draw such
conclusions. Here, in 3:8, he does not at first refute this
reproach but meets it with a strong defense and strikes it
down as if in anger. He does not start a dispute at all but
proclaims judgment on such frivolity. Such talk is blas-
phemy and the sentence must merely be announced to it:
the judgment on it is just.

What does Paul say, then, in this passage? God does not
let himself be caught in the inferences of men. There is
certainly an honest questioning of the heart which stems
from a true search for faith. But if man with his questions
wants to enumerate to God how God is to rule the world
justly, then he becomes not only a fool who thinks he
knows better than God, but finally a blasphemer who wants
to dispute God's justice. Man must realize that he cannot
understand God's possibilities, and must finally be silent
before them. There is finally a point where one can no
longer discuss with the doubter; he can only be warned not
to draw down upon himself the judgment of God for his
calumny.

5 ALL ARE GUILTY AND LOST

3:9–20

3: 9 What then? Are we better off than the Gentiles? Not entirely. For we have just charged that Jews and Greeks are
all under the domination of sin,

10 as it is written,
        "There is not one just man;
11   there is none who understands.
        There is none that seeks after God (Ps 13:1–3).
12   All have gone astray together;
            they have wasted their lives.
        There is none who does good,
            no, not even one (Eccl 7:21; Ps 52:2–4).
13   Their throat is an open sepulcher;
            with their tongues they have dealt deceitfully (Ps
            5:10).
        The venom of asps is behind their lips (Ps 139:4);
14   their mouth is full of bitter curses (Ps 96:7).
15   Their feet run swiftly to the shedding of blood;
16   destruction and misery are in their paths.
17   The highway that leads to peace they have not known
            (Is 59:7f; Prov 1:16).
18   There is no fear of God in their view of things" (Ps
            35:2).
19 Now we know that whatever the Law says, is directed to
        those who come under the Law, in order that every mouth
        may be reduced to silence and the whole world be made
        accountable to God.
20 Obviously by the prescriptions of the Law no human being
        shall be made holy in God's sight, because through law
        comes merely the clearer recognition of sin.

Rom 3:9–20 draws the final conclusions from what has preceded.

(3:9) The Epistle to the Romans has shown that the Gentiles (1:18–32) and the Jews (2:1; 3:9) have fallen into sin and come under the anger of God. Paul has thus brought forward from the history of mankind the proof that all men have fallen to the judgment. They are hopelessly lost.

(3:10–18) Paul now joins to this a confirmation of the

word of God from the Holy Scriptures. From texts of the Old Testament, especially from the Psalms and the Book of Isaias, Paul skillfully fashions a psalm on human sin and depravity. Pupils in rabbinical schools acquired the practice of composing such songs, and Paul undoubtedly learned it there. In its many variations the song of penance reiterates a single theme: if one perceives the true inner nature of man, one finds only guilt and distance from God. Paul has arranged the verses of Scripture, it seems, according to three main ideas: man disregards God and his commandment (3:10–12—stanza a). He destroys the life of his fellow man with his evil tongue (3:13f—stanza b) and on all paths (3:15–18—stanza c).

(3:19) A Jew would be able to say that the verses brought together by Paul speak in the Old Testament of the enemies of the godly, and not of the righteous themselves. But Paul substantiates his procedure. The entire Scripture, as the word of God, concerns in every case the entire people of God. The pious reader of the Bible does not first ask to whom each of the verses was originally addressed. He hears himself personally addressed, directly and inescapably, in every word. And thus the Scripture passes judgment on everyone. "Every mouth is reduced to silence," Paul says. The whole world is under judgment.

(3:20) Thus no man is able to maintain that he can be justified before God by the good works demanded by the law. But then the question finally arises: why is there the law if no one does or can fulfill it? In reality, as the situation is now, it can do nothing but open man's eyes to his state of perdition. It effects only the knowledge of sin, not the conquest of sin; only condemnation, not justification.

In Rom 7 Paul takes up once more the question of the law in order to treat it in detail. The interpretation will also be further developed there.

FOOTNOTES TO CHAPTER II

[1] The Ten Commandments is an ancient and well known catalog of virtues and vices. In comparison with this catalog the list of the Epistle to the Romans is much further developed, unfolded and refined for it not only mentions the gravest sins of commission but distinguishes among sins and also mentions sins of thought and attitudes. The progress through long moral reflection is evident.

[2] The term and concept of conscience are self-evident to us all. But neither the Old Testament nor the gospels use this word, whereas Paul uses it frequently. On the other hand the conscience is spoken of in numerous other texts of that period, especially in Greek literature. Paul has evidently introduced the word from there into the Christian vocabulary.

III REDEMPTION THROUGH JESUS CHRIST

3: 21—8: 39

No man is justified by his own works. The law is powerless to help. Everyone therefore stands under judgment. This is the conclusion of the first section of the Epistle to the Romans, 1:18—3:20. But it is not the last word that Paul has to say, for it is not the law he has to preach but the gospel. And the gospel reveals and brings the justification which God gives.

1 JUSTIFICATION GIVEN THROUGH FAITH IN JESUS CHRIST

3: 21–31

3:21 But now, however, the sanctification brought about by God independently of the Law, yet attested by the Law and the Prophets, has been made manifest:
  22 it is the sanctification brought about by God through faith in Jesus Christ. It comes to all believers, as there is no discrimination.
  23 All have sinned and lack the approval of God.
  24 They are sanctified freely by his grace through the redemption which is in Christ Jesus.
  25 God has publicly exhibited him as a means of expiation available to all through the shedding of his blood. God's

purpose was to vindicate his holiness, since, during the
period of tolerance, he had passed over former sins without punishing them.

26 A further purpose was to make known his holiness at the
present time in sanctifying him who has faith in Jesus.

27 Where, then, is any reason for boasting? It is excluded. By
what kind of law? That of legal prescriptions? No, but by
the law of faith.

28 For we hold that a man is sanctified by faith independently of the deeds prescribed by the Law.

29 Is God the God of the Jews only, and not of the Gentiles
too? Assuredly he is also the God of the Gentiles.

30 Why, there is but one God who will sanctify the circumcised in consequence of their faith and the uncircumcised
by their faith.

31 Do we, therefore, by this faith abolish the Law? By no
means! Rather we uphold the Law.

The turning point of time is at hand. All man's injustice
finds its end in the holy justification of God, which is now
revealed.

(3:21) This revelation happens not only through the
word, so that man would be taught about it, nor does it
happen as perhaps one man out of a thousand could
experience it mystically in the most sublime experience of
God. It is rather a visible event come to pass as an act of
God, that is, in the cross of Christ (3:25). Justification
comes from God, not through the efforts of man, who
stands under the condemnation of the law, which was not
and would not be able to justify anyone. This way of justification is something absolutely new vis-à-vis the law, yet
no break in the word and plan of God. Paul already said in
1:2 that the message of the Old and New Testaments is
the same. In many an interpretation of the Old Testament
in the Epistle to the Romans Paul will further show how

the law and the prophets point forward to the new way of justification; for example, in the story of Abraham, 4:1–25. It is important for Paul to establish this fact in his argument with Israel. He shows thereby that the Old Testament stands on his side and bears witness against unbelieving Israel, which appeals in vain to the Old Testament. But it is also important for him because the unity and truth of the word of God would become questionable if God changed his plans.

(3:22) Justification is given to all the faithful through their faith—faith as the condition of justification is mentioned twice and cannot be ignored. In Rom 4 Paul will explain and interpret what faith is. But for now it is stated: the only condition is that man put his complete trust in what took place in Christ and which is now real; that man thus dare to live from the fact that Christ is there for him. And this condition applies to all who believe, i.e. to Jews and to Gentiles. Here there is no distinction.

(3:23) All were certainly in the same circumstances of sin. Nothing of the glory which God gives to men with sanctification could be found in a single one of them.

(3:24) The justification previously lacking is now given to man, as a gift, without his merit. Nevertheless, grace is not frivolous indulgence or arbitrariness of divine whim— let the heathen idol be changeable. The motive is rather the saving work of Christ. He is and brings about the ransom and redemption of man. One of Jesus' own sayings describes his service in this way (Mk 10:45): "Why, even the Son of Man did not come into the world to be served but to serve and to give his life as a ransom for many." Still further

back, the Old Testament already knows God as the Redeemer (Ps 110:9; 129:7). The prototype of all redemption
is the deliverance of Israel out of Egypt's slavery. But from
what does Christ's death redeem? According to the theology
of Paul and of the entire New Testament, it redeems from
the fate of sin, of the devil, of death, in which man was
hopelessly entangled.

(3:25) With momentous words Paul speaks further of
the death of Christ. The cross is raised as a sign and sacrifice
of atonement between heaven and earth. Paul explains the
cross with an Old Testament expression and image. In the
community of the old covenant, that which was in need of
expiation was not allowed to remain inexpiated. In numerous rites and sacrifices the priests and high-priests were
to cleanse continually the people from its guilt and recon-
cile it with God. When they sprinkled the people with the
blood from the sacrificial animal, the guilt of the sacrificing
people was to be covered before the eyes of God and ex-
piated. Thus the cross is a sacrifice, truly *the* great sacrifice
of atonement. This expiatory work of the cross is brought
about by God himself, however, and is therefore the gift of
God. It is not as if an angry God were reconciled—that
would be conceived in all too human terms. Rather, God's
will to salvation precedes everything.

But also revealed in the cross was God's holiness, the
holiness of the God who cannot simply overlook evil but
denies and judges it, the holiness of the God who sanctifies,
for God's Son interceded for sinners and bore their guilt.
For "Christ redeemed us from the curse threatened by the
law, when he became the object of a curse for us" (Gal

3:13). And "for our sakes God made sin of him who knew no sin, so that in him we might become God's holiness" (2 Cor 5:12). For a long while God had let the sins previously committed go unpunished and had restrained himself as if in patience. God's strict justice could have been thereby obscured. But now the expiation was performed. It benefits him who avails himself of it in faith, who knows that Christ's death is a death of atonement that also concerns him and his sin, and who, embracing the cross, abandons himself to God's judgment and justification.

(3:27) To be sure man is now justified before God. But he cannot pride himself on his justification for it is not his own deed and accomplishment, but is given to him.

(3:28) That man cannot boast applies first of all to the Jew, who would perhaps like to boast about the works of the law which he has accomplished. But it then applies to all human works in general, and Paul is by all means correctly understood if for clarity one translates here: "We hold that a man is sanctified by faith *alone*, independently of the deeds prescribed by the Law."[1] Of course this faith is never merely a confession of faith, but rather that entire faith which finds its expression in love (see under 2:16). But then the words of Saint Theresa of the Child Jesus hold good: "In the evening of my life I will appear before you with empty hands. Our sanctification is full of flaws in your eyes. Thus I want to clothe myself with your sanctification."

(3:29f) If only one could be justified by the works of the law the Jew would be preferred. But God governs over all men with the same care. He is also the God of the

Gentiles. Thus the way of salvation must be one and the same for all. And it can only be faith.

(3:31) Paul listens to still another objection which was once made to him and is still made to this day (similar to the objection in 3:8). He has said that the law is in the end capable of nothing, and that only God's grace gives justification. But it was nevertheless God who gave the law. And this law was Israel's ordinance, salvation and pride since the time of her ancestors. It is a question not only of the law of the Old Testament but of law in general. Is not all law devalued and abolished by Paul's words? Is his teaching not the beginning of disorder and lack of discipline? But Paul replies that he is not abolishing the law but establishing it. He has really established all the earnestness of the law in that he disclosed how the law makes man guilty before God. Faith believes in Christ, who experienced the penal earnestness of the law bodily on the cross and bore it till the end (3:25). And Paul will add that he who believes fulfills for the first time the sense of the law, which is faith (4:1–25) and love (13:10).

2   FAITH AS THE SENSE
OF THE OLD COVENANT

4: 1–25

4: 1 What, then, shall we say that Abraham, our father according to flesh, acquired?

   2 If Abraham was sanctified in consequence of his deeds, he has reason to boast. But it is not so in the sight of God.

3 What does the Scripture say? "Abraham believed God and it was credited to him as holiness" (Gen 15:6).

4 Now to him who works, the pay is not credited as a favor but as something due.

5 But to him who does not work, but believes in him who imparts holiness to the impious, his faith is credited to him as holiness.

6 Thus David declared the blessedness of the man to whom God credits holiness without deeds:

7   "Blessed are they whose breaches of the Law are forgiven and whose sins are blotted from sight;

8   Blessed is the man to whom the Lord will not credit sin" (Ps 31:1f).

9 Does this declaration of blessedness hold good, then, only for the circumcised, or for the uncircumcised also? We say that to Abraham faith was credited as holiness.

10 How, then, was it credited? After he was circumcised or before? Not after he was circumcised, but while he was still uncircumcised.

11 He received circumcision as the seal of the holiness which comes from faith. He had this holiness before he was circumcised, that he might be the father of all who believe, even though uncircumcised, and thus have their faith credited to them as holiness.

12 He will also be the father of the circumcised, provided they are not merely circumcised but direct their steps in the path of that faith which was our father Abraham's before he was circumcised.

13 Not through any law but through the holiness that comes from faith was the promise made to Abraham and to his posterity that he should be the heir of the world.

14 Now if they are heirs in virtue of the Law, faith becomes meaningless, the promise is reduced to nought.

15 The Law produces wrath; for where there is no law, there is no transgression.

16 Therefore the promise was the outcome of faith, in order that it might be a favor and might be secure for all the offspring, not only for those who are adherents of the Law,

but also for those who share the faith of Abraham, who is
the father of us all,

17 as it is written, "I have appointed you the father of many
nations" (Gen 17:5). He is our father in the sight of God,
whom he believed, who gives life to the dead and calls into
existence what was not before.

18 Abraham, hoping against hope, believed, so that he became the father of many nations, according to what was
said,
      "So shall your offspring be" (Gen 15:5).

19 He did not let his faith weaken as he considered his own
body with its already withered vitality, as he was almost a
hundred years old, and the withered vitality of Sara's
womb.

20 In the light of God's promise, he did not waiver in unbelief, but was strengthened in faith. Thus he gave glory
to God,

21 by his strong conviction that whatever God has promised
he is able to carry out.

22 Therefore his faith was credited to him as holiness.

23 Not for his sake alone was it written that "it was credited
to him,"

24 but for our sake also, to whom it will be credited if we
believe in him who raised Jesus our Lord from the dead,

25 who was delivered up for our sins, and rose again for our
sanctification.

Paul has said repeatedly (1:17; 3:21) that the Holy
Scripture of the Old Testament bears witness to his
gospel. Now he draws from the story of Abraham—of
whose sanctification every Jew was convinced—the fact that
even Abraham, according to the account in the Old Testament, did not earn sanctification by his own merit but
received it as a gift of God.

    (4:1–3) If Abraham had earned sanctification by his

own merit he would have had the right to boast about it before God. But nowhere does the Scripture say such a thing. Rather Paul reads there (Gen 15:6) that it was by grace that Abraham's faith was credited to him as holiness.

(4:4f) In the case of work one does not speak of crediting by grace. Rather the due reward is paid out to work.

(4:6) Thus from the story of Abraham it follows: he did not boast of his work, but merely remained steadfast in his faith in God, who makes the godless man just, and this faith was credited to him as holiness.

(4:7f) Paul interrupts his scriptural demonstration from the story of Abraham and supports it with evidence from Ps 31:1f. Here, to be sure, the psalmist is not speaking expressly of sanctification. But that man is blessed whose sins God has forgiven. Yet nowhere is it stated that this sinner is sanctified because of his works. God thus makes him holy and just by his free grace and without regard for the merits of the man. Thus the psalm also bears witness to sanctification without works.

(4:9f) Paul continues the interpretation of the story of Abraham. The statement that Abraham was sanctified without works is still further confirmed to the effect that he was also found just without circumcision. Paul appeals to the fact that Scripture reports Abraham's sanctification (i.e. as early as Gen 15:6) before his circumcision (i.e. not before Gen 17:10f). It is thereby shown that circumcision and the law do not bring about sanctification at all.

(4:11) Paul also concludes this from the account in Genesis, inasmuch as circumcision is mentioned there (Gen 17:10f) as the sign and seal of Abraham's holiness. Thus

Abraham was not in any way sanctified by circumcision. Rather circumcision is only the subsequent seal on the sanctification already given him through faith.

(4:12) God had his reason for this ordering of the story of Abraham. He was thinking of the Gentiles, to whom he wanted some day to give the gift of sanctification for the sake of faith, just as he had given it to Abraham. Abraham is the father of all believers. The Jew was both proud and confident because he had Abraham as a father. The Jew retains the title of honor as the son of Abraham, but Abraham is also the father of all the Gentiles who believe as Abraham believed before his circumcision.

(4:13) To the previous evidence that Abraham was sanctified without works (4:1-8) and without circumcision (4:9-12) Paul adds one last proof (4:13-22), that he was further blessed by God because of his faith. For Paul this follows from the story of the promise and birth of Abraham's son, Isaac (Gen 17, 21). Abraham, hoping against all hope, had faith in the promise of God. According to Gen 18:18 and 22:18, Abraham received the promise that all peoples of the earth were to be blessed in him. Paul, like the Jewish exegetes before him (thus also Sir 44:19ff), understood this as a promise to Abraham that the inheritance of the world would belong to his posterity. Nowhere is it stated, however, that this inheritance was promised to him because of a fulfillment of the law.

(4:14f) The reception of the inheritance could not have been made dependent, for Abraham and his posterity, on the fulfillment of the law, for no one can fulfill the law. For this reason it works only anger, and thus is never a means of reaching God's salvation. If the promise and the inheritance were only to be fulfilled when the law had been fulfilled the inheritance would never be reached.

(4:16) For this reason the promise must rest on faith and grace. Only thus is it certain. Only thus can the blessing hold good for the whole posterity of Abraham, for both Jews and Gentiles. If the promise were a question of the fulfillment of the law the Gentiles, who do not have the Old Testament law, would naturally be excluded from the beginning.

(4:17–19) For Abraham, as the father of all believers, both Jews and Gentiles, the promise that he is to be the father of many nations (Gen 17:5) is now fulfilled. He became the father of nations because he had faith, in contradiction to all naturally possible expectation. Paul recalls how great Abraham's faith must have been if he believed the promise that he would be the father of many nations. For when he received this promise he had as yet no son. He was a hundred years old and his power of procreation was dried up, as was Sara's womb. How then was that promise ever to come true? Against all human impossibility Abraham placed the "nevertheless" of his faith. Therefore Paul designates the God Abraham believed in as he who raises the dead to life and calls that which has no being as if it already existed.[2] Man can only call what exists but God can call what does not exist. When he calls it it comes into existence and is there. The faith of Abraham represents faith as it always is. It is risk against all humanly natural probability. Faith stands always anew before death and nothingness. It is always faith in him who creates out of nothing and raises from the dead.

(4:20–22) The tale of Abraham in Genesis reports that Abraham saw the natural impossibility of the promise of a son. "And as Abraham fell prostrate, he laughed and said to himself, 'Shall a son be born to one who is a hundred years old?'" (Gen 17:17). Paul does not consider this statement a doubt of faith. Faith is not insincere dreaming, therefore. It is not self-deception, which sees or would like to have things otherwise than they are. Veracity of faith is not doubt in faith. On the contrary, Abraham's faith only became strong and genuine by standing against all probability. To Abraham's faith, as to all faith, nothing was given but the word of God. Faith is the confidence that God is powerful enough to carry out his promise. That is giving glory to God, and the fact that Abraham gave glory to God became his sanctification before God.

(4:23) Paul has interpreted the story of Abraham to us. He establishes fundamentally that the Bible does not speak of the past at all but deals continually with our own concerns. Thus in the example of Abraham's faith it became clear what faith is in general.

(4:24) Paul accentuates the main point of comparison. Abraham's faith stood face to face with death just as our faith stands face to face with death. Abraham believed in the God who brings the dead to life; Christians believe in the God who raised the Lord Jesus from the dead. The Christian's own dying is contained in the death of Jesus. The Christian also, in face of death—the death of the Lord as well as his own perpetual death—believes in life. For him too faith means receiving the gift of life in face of death.

(4:25) Faith in life is also, in a true and profound manner, the sanctifying faith of the Christian. From death in sin he obtains the God-given life of sanctification. The sudden change from death to life results according to and by virtue of the death of Christ, who atoned for sin; according to and by virtue of Christ's resurrection, which is the new life. Sanctification is thus based on the death and resurrection of Christ, and the faith that sanctifies is the faith of Easter.

Our modern interpretation, working with methods not available to Paul, may deviate somewhat from the interpretation which he has given to the story of Abraham in Genesis. It cannot but acknowledge, however, that in essence Paul understood correctly the sense and spirit of the story and the significance of the figure of Abraham in the history of salvation. On God's word Abraham left his home in Ur, in Chaldaea, and set out, "awaiting the city with foundations whose architect and builder is God" (Hebr 11:8–10). Thus Paul always represents Abraham as one who has no resting place here, but lives from promise to promise, and as the homeless one who is turned toward the future. And finally, Abraham is the sacrificing one for on the mountain of Moria he is prepared to sacrifice his son, the single bearer of the promise, knowing that "God has power to raise men from the dead" (Hebr 11:19). In both cases faith is the same attitude and action of man who, called by the word of God, lives on the strength of God's gift, always ready to let go of life in order to obtain it.

3 CHRIST: BASIS OF THE NEW WAY OF JUSTIFICATION

5: 1–21

5: 1 Having, therefore, been sanctified by faith, let us have peace with God through our Lord Jesus Christ,

2 through whom also we have found entrance into this state of grace in which we now abide, and exult in the hope of participating in God's glory.

3 Not only this, but we exult in tribulations also, aware that tribulation produces endurance,

4 and endurance proven faith, and proven faith hope.

5 And this hope does not disappoint, because God's love is poured forth in our hearts by the Holy Spirit who has been given to us.

6 While we were still helpless, Christ at the appointed time died for us wicked people.

7 Why, it is only with difficulty that a person will die to save a good man. Yes, it is only for a worthy person that a man may, perhaps, have the courage to face death.

8 But God proves his love for us, because, when we were still sinners, Christ died for us.

9 Much more now that we are sanctified by his blood shall we be saved through him from God's avenging justice.

10 Surely, if when we were enemies we were reconciled to God by the death of his Son, much more, once we are reconciled, shall we be saved by his life.

11 And more than this, we exult also in God through our Lord Jesus Christ, through whom we have now received this reconciliation.

12 Therefore, as through one man sin entered into the world and through sin death, and thus death has spread to all men because all have sinned—

13 true it is that until the Law sin was in the world, but sin is not imputed when there is no law.

14 Yet death held sway from Adam until Moses even over
those who had not sinned after the manner of the transgression of Adam, a type of him who was to come.

15 But the gift is not at all like the offense. For if by the
offense of the one the many died, much more has the
grace of God, and the gift which consists in the grace of
the one man, Jesus Christ, overflowed unto the many.

16 Nor is the gift as it was in the case of the one man's sin,
for the judgment unto condemnation followed the one
man's offense, but grace resulting in sanctification follows
many offenses.

17 For if by reason of the one man's offense death reigned
through the one man, much more will they who receive
the abundance of the grace and of the gift of holiness
reign in life through the one Jesus Christ.

18 Therefore as from the offense of the one man the result
was condemnation to all men, so from the one's fulfillment
of a mandate the result is the sanctification which gives
life to all men.

19 In other words, just as by the disobedience of the one
man the many were constituted sinners, so also by the
obedience of the one the many will be constituted holy.

20 The Law intervened that the offense might become greater.
But the greater the offense became, so much the more has
grace increased.

21 So, just as sin has resulted in the reign of death, so also
grace, which confers holiness leading to eternal life, holds
sway through Jesus Christ our Lord.

The new justification has its foundation and its fullness
in Christ. Paul speaks first of all of the individual gifts
which are given with justification or promised for the future (5:1–11), and then recapitulating everything, describes
justification as the new life of a new humanity.

(5:1) Peace is mentioned as the first gift. Peace (as in
1:7) is the order of salvation between God and the

world. As a sinner man stood opposed to God, and God to man. Now an end has been put to the discord. Those justified by faith are at peace with God. The word peace, the word of blessing and longing continually repeated in the Old Testament, is now fulfilled. According to Is 9:5, the Messiah is to be the Prince of Peace. And Paul now says that Jesus Christ is the awaited author of this peace. It is certain that this peace, after its objective establishment, also becomes the personal experience and consciousness of the believer.

(5:2) In Christ the Lord the entrance to the grace of sanctification is gained, and through it the entrance to the Father, as Paul says elsewhere (Eph 2:18; 3:12) in continuing the thought and image. The image is similar in Jn 10:9, where Jesus calls himself the door through which the sheep enter into salvation. Judging from the wording, Paul seems to be using the image of a liturgical procession. He sees the beginning of the great procession of the Church, marching into the Kingdom of God from all zones and all ages. Every believer in the great procession has the right to go to the Father, as a son into his father's house. Every Christian, as a member of the community, has the right to direct relationship with God. Using another image, it can also be said that the believer stands fast on the foundation of the act of God. The Christian has, in fact, a new standing, the "Christian state." He is not yet at home, but what is given to him is the surety of what is greater still, and yet to come. The final goal of the road which faith has begun to walk on is the glory of God. This hope is already the glory and splendor of the Christian. Paul said in 3:27 that all boasting is excluded. But now there is nonetheless a reason for boasting—not one's own act, but the promised and anticipated gift of God.

(5:3f) Present tribulations cannot oppress or stifle this boast at all. Paul is certainly not able to say that the Christian boasts of tribulations—that would be grandiloquence. Yet he does say that the Christian exults in tribulation, whereby he prides himself not on his own power but on the power of God. This power becomes effective in man's weakness and in the life of God revealed in the death of man (2 Cor 4:9f). He who boasts in this way does not gaze upon himself but away from himself, toward God. So tribulation does not mean defeat for faith, but rather firmness and strength in the sequence: endurance, proven faith, hope. This endurance does not mean resignedly accommodating oneself to the situation, but the knowing, active abiding which subsists on the promise of God. The greater the endurance the greater the proof of faith. Every proof of faith anticipates the final complete victory. Therefore the greater the test the greater the hope. The words and phrases are like a chain in which one link is firmly attached to the next.

(5:5) The chain is safely suspended from its last link, the love of God. This love of God is not—in any case not primarily and originally—the pious man's love of God, but God's love for man. God has taken the first step and he will not abandon man. The Christian has experienced this divine love overwhelmingly in the Holy Spirit, whom the love of God has poured forth abundantly over the Church and over each believer. The Holy Spirit obtains for us the love of God, just as in Jn 14:26; 16:13 it is his task to complete the work of Christ.

Everything hangs on the love of God, that is, on the fact that God is not a god inferred by philosophy as the supreme being, but rather he who loves. This is the guarantee for the entire chain on which the life of man hangs. For this reason the Christian will never stand in disgrace in the judgment. (We note that in these verses Paul mentions faith, hope and love together, one after the other. He has already enumerated them in this way in the Epistle to the Corinthians, written in the previous year [1 Cor 13:13]: "So now we have these three, faith, hope, and love, but the greatest of them is love.")

(5:6f) Verses 5:6–11[3] intend to prove that the love of God is greater than all things. The proof is furnished by the reflection that if God has done so much for sinners, what will he not do for the justified and the beloved!

Christ died for us when we were still weak, i.e. incapable of doing good, even impious. All the more surely will God's love be with the just. It will not happen among men that a precious life is given up for a worthless one. Humanly possible is at best death for a good friend.

(5:8) But such an exceptional case of heroism is not under consideration here. God acted altogether differently. He sacrificed Christ for godless men. This proves the magnitude of his love, which did not give man up for lost. Through sanctification it made worthy of love those who were not worthy. Thus the extreme purity of God's love is revealed—a love which bestows groundlessly.

(5:9) God gave his love to sinners. How much more will

it now belong to the just. Christ will not condemn in the judgment those who are justified in his blood. Paul knows Christ as the Judge in the last judgment (cf. 2:16), as he also says in 2 Cor 5:10: "We must all be laid open to inspection before the tribunal of Christ." So also the gospels expect Christ as the Judge of the world. "The Son of Man is to come hereafter wrapt in his Father's glory and escorted by his angels; and then he will repay everyone according to his conduct" (Mt 16:27). "Nor, again, does the Father judge anyone; no, the right to judge he has turned over wholly to the Son" (Jn 5:22). In 5:9 Paul sketches a scene of judgment. Everyone appears in the judgment, for the just also stand in the anger, i.e. the judgment of God. They are not saved in such a way that they would not be called to account. Rather they experience salvation in the midst of judgment.

(5:10) Once more Paul infers the great from the small, and this in a double sense. If even the enemies of God experienced atonement, how much more will the atoned receive salvation. And if the death of the Son of God brought about the atonement, how much more will his life now guarantee final salvation.

Paul thus describes the fruits of the death of Jesus as atonement. He uses thereby—as in 3:25—a concept and an expression of Old Testament and late Jewish teaching and expectation. Israel celebrated and celebrates annually to this day the great Day of Atonement (Yom Kippur), when the entire people was absolved. So that the glory of God could then reside among them, Israel's expectation, Paul says, has now been fulfilled. The cross brings about once and for all the true and final atonement. But this is done not in the sense that God would be won over and appeased —pagan religions, to be sure, may have this conception of their gods. Rather in biblical faith sinners are reconciled with God, who creates a new relationship between himself and the world and gives sinners the possibility of grasping the atonement given by God. The change which occurs in the atonement is thus not on God's part but always on our part, on the part of men, as the text (5:10) twice states: we were reconciled. It further establishes that we cease being weak and wicked (5:6), sinners (5:8) and enemies (5:10).

(5:11) We have not only confidence in future salvation, but even now the certainty of God's consummating love. Here one has the right to boast (see also 5:3f). He who boasts, boasts not of himself but of God. Christ the Lord, who was the Mediator of salvation in the present, will be that and still much more in the future. He will intercede for those whom he reconciled with God also in the judgment. The confidence of the Christian is thus not based on his own virtue but on the faithfulness of God. Everything stems finally from the love of God (5:5). Our passage also deals forcibly with everyday tribulations and the moral attitudes necessary in them, with peace and endurance, with the testing of faith and hope. But they are not to be understood principally as virtues, and the epistle does not exhort us to acquire and practice them. Rather they are gifts and acts of God for man which the apostle has to proclaim. To this extent here also is gospel, the praise of the work of God.

(5:12) In a phrase which declares the theme of the epistle Paul has said (1:17): "The holy man lives by faith." Life is promised as the fruit of salvation. Paul now explains (5:12–21) what this life is all about. He does so with a vast confrontation of Adam as the very beginning of life— to be sure also the beginning of death—and Christ as the new beginning and the consummation of life.

The apostle's language in these verses is extraordinarily fussy, even more so in the original Greek than in our smoother translation. Sentences once begun are broken off, taken up once again, complicated by intervening questions, then corrected. The thought process is at first not easy to understand. The language is not suitable because the subject is not suited to human calculation. Where God is concerned, human estimation will always fall short of the mark.

Paul proceeds from the story of the fall as related in Genesis 2 and 3 and further interprets the ancient tale just as, in fact, Jewish theology of his time did. Genesis tells how Adam and Eve were struck by the punishment of death because they violated the divine prohibition. It intends to explain thereby that death reigns in the world ever since as the punishment for sin. Since that time all men stand under the fate of death. Following this teaching, for example, Wisd 2:23f says: "God formed man to be imperishable . . . But by the envy of the devil, death entered into the world." So also does Paul now teach that death spread from the first man and his sin to all men. All inherited death from Adam. Death is thus hereditary.

Exegesis on the Epistle to the Romans has gone to a

great deal of trouble to determine whether Paul also teaches that as a result of original sin all men, as children of Adam, enter the world burdened by the sin inherited from him. Yet a careful interpretation of the text indicates that Paul does not teach a doctrine of original sin with the same clarity as does the later and present doctrinal theology of the Church. Rather Paul emphasizes—at any rate in 5:12; but cf. 5:18f below—the personal guilt and sin of each of Adam's children. The flow of sin certainly proceeds from Adam but all men enter into this flow with personal decision and guilt. From this, their own sin, the fate proceeding from Adam comes into effect for those who are born later. "Death has spread to all men because all have sinned." Exegesis notes that Jewish theology of that time perhaps taught death by inheritance, but hardly original sin. For instance, the Apocalypse of Baruch, written about 100 A.D., reads (54:15): "Only for himself is Adam the cause of sin and death. But all of us, each man became an Adam for himself." Yet the faith of Israel lives in the expectation that history, which stands under the mark of an original, disastrous event, is moving toward and aiming at a final saving event. Just as will the Church of the New Testament (Paul, in 5:14), so according to Daniel 7 does pious Israel already await the coming of the Son of Man, who will bring general renewal.

(5:13f) With the thought processes which he had learned in the school of Jewish theology Paul proves that by virtue of the racial unity with Adam, death, as his inheritance, proceeded to all men. Adam had drawn down upon himself the penalty of death by his violation of the commandment given in paradise. Moses then, and for the first time, gave Israel commandment and law again. From Adam to Moses there was certainly sin but nowhere in this period was violation of the law placed under the penalty of death. And yet men also died between the time of Adam and the time of Moses. They did not die because they were deserving of death by virtue of the law; rather their death was the result of the first sin of the one Adam. Paul finally mentions Adam as a type of he who was to come, i.e. of the Messiah. Adam points beyond himself toward Christ. The guilt of Adam has called forth the salvation through another, the Christ. That the act of an individual can have such a decisive effect for everybody—precisely therein is Adam the type of what took place in Christ. "Just as in Adam all men die, so too in Christ all men are brought to life" (1 Cor 15:22).

Paul proves his point in the manner and style customary in his time. We can perhaps not follow him step by step. But independent of such historical limitations, the biblical and Christian belief regarding death is here expressed. "Death entered into the world through sin" (5:12). Death, as all life in the world today suffers it, does not belong to the original creation of God. How would this be possible since God is the Creator of life, and so cannot be its destroyer? Death does not reign in the world as an ordinance and occurrence of nature. It is not only a wearing out of the body, not only a breaking down of the cells, not only a natural waxing and waning of life; it is a punishment. (On the question of whether God had the right to burden mankind with the weight of such an inheritance, see under 5:18

below.) Death is therefore not the friend of man but his enemy. Man is subject to this enemy to the last. "The last enemy to be destroyed will be death" (1 Cor 15:26). The New Testament thereby characterizes death as it truly is and as it is experienced—naturally, at any rate—by man: as an enemy. It destroys life, and destruction can never be man's friend. Death is here seen in its reality; nothing is suppressed and kept secret. The New Testament is capable of seeking and bearing reality because it can proclaim, in the face of this reality, the confidence and hope that man is not left alone in death but is led through death into life. For the power of the Lord never abandons him. "We shall continue in the Lord's company forever. Therefore encourage one another with these words" (1 Thess 4:17f).

(5:15) As Paul pursues the comparison between Adam and Christ (5:15–21), he continually interrupts himself and says that there is really no equalizing the two because they are truly incomparable. God's grace and life must certainly surpass all the destiny of sin that stems from Adam. God would not be God if his salvatioin were not incomparably greater and stronger than all calamity.

Adam and Christ do correspond to one another inasmuch as each represents the whole race. Adam is the original man and all men are his children. So it is comprehensible that his figure and his story became the story of all. But likewise Christ contains within himself a new humanity, which begins with him. In the intellectual history of mankind Christ is a noble moral thinker and teacher, in the history of religion a founder of a religion. In Paul's teaching, however—and it is, alone, the complete Christian teaching—

Christ is something altogether different. Christ is more than the great forefathers and prophets of Israel; more also than Moses, the greatest man in Israel, the prince of the people and the friend of God. If another is to be compared to him it can only be Adam, the progenitor of humanity. If Adam is the beginning so also is Christ the new beginning of mankind. Both are destinies for the entire human race. Through both were decisions made for all—though they were altogether contrary decisions. On the one hand the end is sin and death; on the other justification and life. Beginning with Christ all humanity is new humanity. Paul speaks of Adam and Christ in 1 Cor 15:45–49 in much the same way as in Rom 5:12–21. There he shows how the restoration in Christ is more than the origin in Adam. The creation in Adam pointed beyond itself from the very beginning toward the new creation in Christ. The first man, Adam, as Paul says, was "of dust" and a "soul having life." He waited from the very beginning for the second man, who is "from heaven" and a "spirit imparting life." Christ is not only redemption from the fall but the consummation of creation; not only restoration but the exaltation of the first man. With such a view of Christ as the mid-point and summation of the entire creation, Paul can say: "We, the aggregate, are one body in Christ" (12:5). And he understands in this depth the formulas which he often uses: "in Jesus Christ" and "in the Lord."

(5:16) Adam and Christ are really to be compared with one another. And yet, how could condemnation and acquittal be measured against one another! In the verdict it is strictly a question of right and law—the more exact, the more just. Thus sentence is passed on the basis of sin and leads to condemnation. It is different with grace, where sanctification is not calculated but freely given for sin. And sanctification is abundantly sufficient for all sins, no matter how numerous.

(5:17) The power of life is stronger than the power of death. Even if death, like a king, exercised sovereign power, how much different the dominion of life will be. The just will reign royally in life with Christ. Once men were slaves of the tyrant death; henceforth they will be kings in life.[4]

(5:18f) Paul summarizes the results of the confrontation up to this point: in each case there is one person as cause and origin, Adam and Christ; in each case, one act, sin and justification, disobedience and obedience; in each case, consequences for all humanity, for disaster and for salvation.

Just as we found in 5:12 the teaching about death as an inheritance from Adam, so also is the idea of original sin hinted at by Paul in 5:18f. If in 5:12 he said that all men by sinning entered into the flow of sin stemming from Adam, so now he says that the destiny of sin had its effect from Adam on; further, through Adam's disobedience all men became sinners (5:19), and through Adam's guilt all are condemned (5:18). Paul does not use the term original sin. He distinguishes between the destiny stemming from Adam and each man's personal decision for evil, through which that destiny becomes real, personal sin. But the teaching on original sin which developed in the western Latin Church (the eastern Greek Church took little part in the development of this teaching) is based on Paul. Our

modern Church dogma retains that distinction between
original sin and actual, personal sin. It also says that the
same word, sin, means something different in the two
instances. It differentiates sin as fateful inheritance and
sin as an act to be accounted for. Accordingly the (penal)
consequences are also different.[5]

The biblical and Church teaching on original sin is perhaps not immediately comprehensible to us. How is so
strange and distant a guilt supposed to be fateful for all
future generations? For both natural and biblical thinking, but in a way different from Christian thinking, it is
an understandable, even familiar truth that the individual
is fixed within the whole race and is bound as its member
to the great community, whether for disaster or for salvation. In the Ten Commandments it states (Ex 20:5f):
"For I, the Lord, your God, am a jealous God, inflicting
punishment for their fathers' wickedness on the children
of those who hate me, down to the third and fourth gen-
eration; but bestowing mercy down to the thousandth gen-
eration, on the children of those who love me and keep my
commandments." Thus the first readers of the Epistle to
the Romans probably understood this teaching of the community of death stemming from Adam, and also of the
community of life proceeding from Christ, more directly
and more easily than us today. Yet it only tells us didacti-
cally what we experience daily: that the commandment to
do good always meets in us a reluctant human being. Good
always demands first a renunciation of evil. This renunciation signifies and reveals that man has always lived in sin.

(5:20) The two verses 5:20f are a comment especially

on 5:13f. Paul said that Adam and Christ are the two poles and the two epochs of the history of mankind. "The law intervened." For Jews the law is a new epoch in the history of the world. What is, then, the significance of the law? This is the unchanging Jewish question which nonetheless also occupies Paul. Does the law have no decisive significance? No, at any rate none which would be comparable to the epochs of Adam and Christ! As something additional, the law came into the history of the world and intensified the destiny of sin and death proceeding from Adam (cf. under 4:15). It was not capable of stemming the flow of sin. Only Christ was capable of that.

(5:21) Yet even the law must serve God's decree of salvation, for the increase in sin can only cause grace to become all the more abundant. The forcible rule of sin and death will finally be relieved by the reign of grace in Christ. Everything proceeds toward this goal.

4 THE NEW LIFE

6: 1–14

6: 1 What then shall we say? Shall we continue in sin that grace may increase? By no means!
2 For how shall we, who are dead to sin, still live in it?
3 Do you not know that all of us who have been baptised into union with Christ Jesus have been baptised into union with his death!
4 Yes, we were buried in death with him by means of Baptism, in order that, just as Christ was raised from the dead by the glorious power of the Father, so we also may conduct ourselves by a new principle of life.

5 Now since we have grown to be one with him through a death like his, we shall also be one with him by a resurrection like his.

6 We know that our old self has been crucified with him, in order that the body enslaved to sin may be reduced to impotence, and we may no longer be slaves to sin;

7 for he who is dead is once for all quit of sin.

8 But if we haved died with Christ, we believe that we shall also live with him,

9 since we know that Christ, having risen from the dead, will die no more; death shall no longer have dominion over him.

10 The death that he died was a death to sin once for all, but the life that he lives is a life for God.

11 Thus you too must consider yourselves dead to sin, but alive to God in Christ Jesus.

12 Do not then let sin reign in your mortal body so as to obey its lusts.

13 And do not go on offering your members to sin as instruments of iniquity, but once for all dedicate yourselves to God as men that have come to life from the dead, and your members as instruments of holiness for God;

14 for sin shall not have dominion over you, since you are not subjects of the Law but of grace.

Justification is the gift of God for man. But it is a creative gift which must become effective in the moral sanctification of life. Rom 6–8 deals with this new life. At the end of these chapters, however, stands not the image of virtuous and pious man, perhaps the portrayal of the highest level which he attained in his strained ascent, but rather the glorification of God's love, with which God maintains men and from which no power is able to separate them. Here again it is not finally the endeavors of man but God's gift of justification which is proclaimed (cf. under 5:11).

(6:1) Paul proceeds from weighty questions which can arise from his gospel. Is not the conclusion from phrases like 3:5 and 5:20: many sins, much grace? Is sin so evil if in the end it makes God's grace greater? Is not sin the necessary gateway to good? Further questions result from 3:24 and 3:28 where it is taught that justification is freely given to faith without works. If our justification is thus not our own doing, is not all human action and endeavor a matter of indifference? Is not the crude phrase finally true: sin strenuously but believe even more strenuously?[6] Paul has already made such objections to himself (see 3:8), and now he makes them again. Perhaps he had to listen to them from opponents who imputed such conclusions to him. Perhaps there were already some who understood Paul's teaching on the law as an invitation to licentiousness. In any case Paul's teaching has occasionally been thus misunderstood and misused in the course of Church history. In fact Paul's true teaching is the mean between two extremes which is not always easy to find and to follow. On the one hand is the temptation to make out of grace a *carte blanche* for evil, or at least to despise sober obedience as the trivial work of man, in order to set up God's grace all the more in power. On the other hand is a thorough moralism which, should one speak too much of the gifts and action of God, will demand works of lawfulness and fears for morality. But it must nevertheless hold true: "You are not subjects of the law but of grace" (6:14).

(6:2) Paul clarifies the questions and refutes the false conclusions by interpreting facts which are acknowledged as indisputable. It is a fundamental truth that Christians have died to sin, since they died with Christ. Their relation to sin is broken off by death. Just as one takes final leave of a man in the grave, so he who has abandoned himself in the death of Christ has taken leave of his earlier self, which was under submission to sin. This has taken place as an act of God for us. Woe to him who despises this work of God by returning to sin. Paul does not admonish with a "you will!" but with a reminder of a "you are!" The moral question is decided by what has happened at the beginning, already, through God's act.

(6:3) When did it take place, this death with Christ to sin? Paul is not thinking of an act of the will or a resolution by which the convert would have promised himself and God henceforth to renounce evil. That death Christians have undergone in baptism. The recipients of the epistle know that this is the sense and content of what takes place in baptism. In baptism the death of Christ is carried out in the believer. He dies with Christ on the cross. Just as the cross was the destruction of the power of sin, so he who is baptised is withdrawn from its power and has broken with it.

(6:4) Paul seems to be thinking of the rite of baptism as it was performed at that time. Baptism was not conferred by pouring water over the head of the baptismal candidate but by immersion of the adult candidate in water. This immersion seems to be an image of burial for the apostle. Thus the Christian has received a symbolic share in the death of Christ. The death of Christ, however, as the death of salvation, is always both his cross and his resurrection (8:34: "It is Jesus Christ who died, yes, and who rose again"). So also the baptismal candidate receives a share both in the death and the resurrection of the Lord. The goal of baptism is life with Christ. The text will have to be precisely interpreted here. If Paul said, we have died with Christ, then the statement, Christ was raised from the dead, would logically be followed by, so were we also raised. But Paul does not say this and he would certainly not be able to say this. Rather he says: so we also may conduct ourselves by a new principle of life. That other statement would have been too uninhibitedly blatant. By virtue of natural events man is born as the child of his parents, to whom he belongs, whether he wants to or not. The new life obtained in baptism is different. It must be grasped in faith and fulfilled in each personal life. For this reason then: so that we may also conduct ourselves by a new principle of life.

(6:5) Paul explains further how baptism gives a share in Christ's death and resurrection. According to the rite of immersion as a burial with Christ, and according to its sense and content as sharing in the cross of Christ, baptism is a representation of Christ's death, veiled in the sacrament. In the execution of the sacrament the baptismal candidates grow to be one with this image of Christ's death and resurrection. Once again Paul does not so express himself that his words could be understood as an affirmation that we are already risen from the dead. Rather he says: we will also share in the resurrection. The consummation is still a promise, even if the future resurrection and the future life of the resurrection already show their powerful presence in the life of the Christian.

(6:6) Paul repeats and clarifies: if baptism represents the death of Christ then being baptised means the crucifixion of the old self with Christ. If the cross of Christ is the putting away of sin then baptism must also be the renunciation of sin. The old self—having nothing in common with the new world and as fallen man stemming from Adam—is condemned. The body of sin, i.e. the man of sin, is executed. Sin in general is overthrown. But once again Paul may not be so understood, as if innocence were henceforth the nature of man and as if there could be no more sin in the Church. Paul immediately continues the statement, to the effect that the compulsion to be a slave to sin is abolished. It is not as if all sin would immediately come to an end, but it is true that the final victory can now be won.

(6:7) For further proof Paul seems to appeal to a legal maxim which, in the Jewish theology of that time, stated: as soon as a man is dead he is free from taxes, free from the law, and free from the fulfillment of the commandments. Thus whoever has died is also acquitted from sin. Now he who is baptised has died and is thus freed from slavery to sin. It has lost all claim on him. Who would want to make this legally unequivocal relationship invalid through renewed service under sin?

(6:8f) We have died with Christ. Thus we believe that we will also live with him. Once more we notice the careful expression. The new life is not given and guaranteed in a natural way but is to be grasped in faith and still hoped for in the future. The future does not mean merely the futurity of eternal life but also the life of the Christian right now, as life stemming from and leading toward the resurrection.

(6:10) Christ stood under sin and sin had a claim on him, for he had become like those who were under the power of death on account of sin. But through his death he has fully and completely discharged what they owed for sin and what he took upon himself in their stead. Now his life belongs to God forever. The decision is made once and for all. There is no possible turning back, neither for Christ nor for those who have died and risen again with him in baptism.

(6:11) Christians must therefore know and understand that, dead to sin, they are to live for God. Again Paul says that this new life is not produced naturally or magically. Rather the Christian must grasp it in understanding. God truly acts on man but only in such a way that God acts with him. Natural life remains as before. The new reality is only real in that it is established in the "neverthless" of faith. The new life is true but hidden in Christ (Col 3:3).

(6:12) The new life is superior to whatever is naturally experienced but it forcibly affects ascertainable reality. This reality is corporeality. The body is mortal, as before. But sin, whose fruit is mortality, may no longer reign in the body.

(6:13) And in the great struggle between sin and justification the baptised must in the future stand on the side of God in life and in death.[7] Otherwise the death and resurrection of God, having taken place in the act of God on man, is deprived of its truth and reality.

(6:14) The law makes demands in order to condemn, in that it always merely calls forth the failure of man and leaves him alone in it. Grace is freedom and capacity to act justly, but for this reason it is also the obligation to do so.

The apostle's sentences describe not only each individual's life between sin and grace, past and future, but also the character of the Church. The newness of life is given to her and instituted in her. But it is not produced and made effective with natural necessity or magic certainty, but only made known in word and sacrament. It must always be grasped in faith and realized in decision and action. The Church lives between the "already" of her present and the "not yet" of her future. She still awaits the final consummation. But both sacrament and ethos belong to the Church. If either is cast aside she is ruined. If the sacrament is considered a magically certain, effective agent and the ethos becomes unimportant, so that the baptised consider themselves the sanctified who can never fall out of favor, then there arises within this "Church of the saints" a sect of improbability and unreality. Here it is forgotten that the consummation is still to be awaited and realized. If the sacrament is depleted and the sacramental reality lost, and in its stead, perhaps, the ethical endeavor intensified to the highest forcefulness, then the Church becomes all too quickly an association for the encouragement of culture, ethics and religion. The Church is certainly this too, but she is something else and something more. Here it is forgotten that the Church is the community of those already redeemed.

5 SLAVERY AND FREEDOM

6: 15–23

6:15 What then? Are we to sin because we are not subjects of the Law but of grace? By no means!

16 Do you not know that when you offer yourselves as slaves to obey anyone, of that one you are the slaves, whether of sin which leads to death or of obedience which leads to holiness?

17 But thanks be to God that you who were the slaves of sin have now wholeheartedly obeyed the kind of teaching you were taught,

18 and after being set free from sin, you have become the slaves of holiness.

19 I am making use of these human analogies out of regard for your weak human nature; for as you offered your members to be slaves of uncleanness and iniquity, culminating in utter wickedness, so now offer your members to be slaves of right living, culminating in holiness.

20 When you were the slaves of sin, you rendered no service to holiness.

21 But what advantage had you then from those things of which you are now ashamed? They finally end in death.

22 But now, set free from sin and become slaves of God, you have your reward in sanctification, which finally leads to life everlasting.

23 For the wages that sin gives is death, but the gift that God bestows is life everlasting in Christ Jesus our Lord.

It seems possible to conclude that freedom from the law is license for sin. But Paul proves the contrary true: the freedom given in the gospel is not merely lack of restraint but a change of master, from sin to rightdoing, from impurity to holiness, from death to life. Freedom from sin is service for God. But precisely this bond is true liberation.

(6:15) Once again Paul takes up the question of 6:1, the question of the relation of law, sin and grace. The repetition indicates how Paul is wrestling with the question.

(6:16) Paul recalls the generally valid law that a slave is subordinated to his master in complete obedience. But with regard to morality man can only choose between two masters, sin or rightdoing. There is no third, and each man must decide one way or the other. It is thus not at all a question of freedom or service; rather a question of service for the one or the other. The one service leads to death, the other to sanctification.

(6:17) But—thanks be to God!—the readers and listeners have chosen. (Paul does not praise them in any way but gives thanks to God, for it was not human capacity that made the choice; rather God gave it.) They were slaves of sin. Sin is only apparent freedom but truly slavery (Jn 8:34: "Everyone who commits sin is the slave of sin"). Now the readers and listeners have become wholeheartedly obedient to the kind of teaching to which they were committed. In a striking way Paul emphasizes that faith and gospel are not feeling, disposition and experience, but the order of teaching and life of the community of the Church. The faithful have been committed to this order. By whom were they committed? The apostle probably means to say that it was God who committed them since he effects the beginning and the consummation of salvation.

(6:18) It is repeatedly stated that it can only be a question of an either-or of servitude. Man cannot throw off this servitude but only alternate it between sin and rightdoing.

(6:19) Paul has now thoroughly expounded the servitude, indeed the slavery of the Christian. And yet his true concern is to say that the situation of the Christian is not slavery but freedom in spirit and sonship before the beloved Father (8:15). For this reason the apostle now almost excuses himself. He says that he is speaking in simile and image of human conditions. He does so because of the weakness of human nature; i.e. since man is in fact tempted and in danger of misunderstanding or even misusing the gospel as a pretext for licentiousness, Paul had to describe the freedom at great length as a new servitude. Yet this truly means freedom from impurity and lawlessness,[8] and freedom for justification and holiness. Justification means first of all the justification given by God, and only then the sanctification effected in one's life. So in this formula holiness must mean first the consecration of man effected by God through call and sacrament, and only then one's own striving for sinlessness.

(6:20) Paul further discloses the previous situation of the Christians as they now understand it. They once considered themselves free in sin, but in truth they were slaves of sin and did not serve holiness.

(6:21f) The contrast between before and now becomes clear if one looks at the proceeds. Now they think of the past with deep shame. Now they know that the end could only be death and judgment. The fruits of the new life, however, are holiness and eternal life.

(6:23) Paul summarizes everything once more in the image of military service, as in 6:13. On the one hand sin is the leader of the host, on the other God is. The soldier receives the pay due him. On the one hand the wage is death, on the other God-given life. But it is no coincidence that Paul does not express himself in this way. Man does earn punishment as his reward but life is never earned by man as a reward. Rather it is always God's gift to man, for the sake of Christ. Therefore Paul instinctively changes the word from wage to gift. Death is wage, life is the gift of grace.

Grace is certainly the end of sterile legality but not the end of the law, if only it is correctly understood as a law of faith (3:27) which obliges one to complete submission to the service of God. The gospel, correctly understood, is therefore not the endangering but rather the foundation of genuine and earnest morality. This morality is not external obligation but the fruit of inner freedom. The old self is executed by God's judgment and action. Therefore the Christian executes that which still belongs to the old self (6:11). The believer is a new creation and therefore renews himself continually (12:2). In the battle victory is already real. The morality of the Christian is acknowledgement of the redemption which has taken place. The preaching of grace does not release man from responsibility but always directs him to that responsibility. In the work of salvation the ever-merciful God is his partner. Should he forget this it would be his ruin. Therefore: "Work out your salvation with fear and trembling. Really it is God who of his good pleasure accomplishes in you both the will and the attainment" (Phil 2:12f).

6 THE OLD LAW

7: 1–25

7: 1 Do you not know, brothers—I am speaking to those who know law—that the Law has dominion over a man as long as he lives?

2 For example, the married woman is bound by the Law while her husband is alive, but if her husband dies, she is free from the law binding her to her husband.

3 Consequently, while her husband is alive, she will be called an adulteress if she unites herself to another man; but if her husband dies, she is set free from the Law, so that she is not an adulteress if she unites herself to another man.

4 Therefore, my brothers, you in turn, through the body of Christ, have died to the Law, to unite yourselves to another, to him who has risen from the dead, in order that we may bring forth fruit for God.

5 While we were in the flesh, sinful passions, aroused by the Law, were at work in our members so that they brought forth fruit for death.

6 But now we have been set free from the Law, having died to that by which we were held down, so that we may render service which is new and according to the spirit, not old and according to the letter.

7 What shall we say, then? Is the Law sin? By no means! Yet I had not known sin save through the Law. For I had not known lust unless the Law had said, "You shall not lust."

8 But sin, having seized a base of operations in the commandment, produced in me by its means all manner of lust, for without law sin lies dormant.

9 Once too I was without law, but when the commandment came, sin was stirred to life,

10 and I died. Thus the commandment that was to lead to life, was discovered in my case to lead to death.

11 Sin, having seized a base of operations in the commandment, deceived me, and thereby killed me.

12 So the Law, surely, is holy and the commandment holy and just and good.

13 Did then that which is good become death to me? By no means! But sin, that it might be manifest as sin, produced death for me through what is good, in order that sin by reason of its abuse of the commandment might become immeasurably sinful.

14 We know well that the Law is spiritual but I am carnal, sold into slavery to sin.

15 Why, I do not understand what I do, for what I wish, I do not; what I hate, I do.

16 But if I do what I do not wish, I admit that the Law is good.

17 But then it is no longer I who do it, but the sin that dwells in me.

18 Well do I know that in me, that is, in my lower nature, no good dwells, because to wish is within my power, but I do not find the strength to accomplish what is good.

19 Yes, I do not do the good that I wish, but the evil that I do not wish, that I do.

20 Now if I do what I do not wish, it is no longer I who do it, but the sin that dwells within me.

21 Therefore, when I wish to do good, I discover this to be the rule, that evil is ready to hand.

22 My inner self agrees joyfully with the Law of God,

23 but I see another law in my bodily members warring against the Law which my mind approves and making me prisoner to the law in my members which allures me to sin.

24 Unhappy man that I am! Who will rescue me from this body doomed to death?

25 Thanks be to God! Through Jesus Christ our Lord (rescue is effected). So then, I by myself with my mind serve

the Law of God, but with my lower nature the law which allures me to sin.

Just as Paul showed in 6:1–14 that Christians have died to sin and are thus free from it, so now (7:1–6) he demonstrates that they have died to the law and are thereby legally redeemed and freed from it. As in other epistles so also in the Epistle to the Romans Paul must deal with the question of the law again and again. So far he has stated: the law brings only knowledge of sin (3:20), only transgression and thence the wrath of judgment (4:15). The law even increases the transgression in order to draw out the revelation of grace in return (5:20). But for this reason the Church can no longer be subject to the law, for to be subject to the law would mean to be subject to sin (6:14). The question is so difficult that Paul takes it up once more in order to present it now in 7:1–25 in all its breadth and depth.

This is all to be understood first from the standpoint of the Jew. To the Jew the law is the regulation of his personal life and of his national community. By means of the law Israel had become a political nation long before many other peoples. She had the law to thank for her pure belief in God in the midst of idolatry on all sides. To the law she owed her intellectual and moral development in the face of the horrible licentiousness among the heathen peoples. Can Israel give up this law without losing her orderliness? And besides, this law is the word and the gift of God. Thus the question is still much more difficult. Can Israel, may Israel separate herself from this law without becoming disobedient and unfaithful to God?

But then the question of the significance of the law becomes of substantial importance to the Church, above and beyond those historical circumstances. The law appears, in general, in the perspectives of the Old Testament Jewish laws. The law stands relentlessly strict against sin, threatens and punishes it. What becomes of man without this discipline? Does not being without law mean being without moral earnestness and order? Does not grace lead one astray to unhesitating sin since grace always forgives and offers a new beginning?

(7:1) For the solution to the question Paul begins once more with the legal maxim, generally acknowledged as valid, to which he has already referred in 6:7: death releases one from the obligation to the law and nullifies the legal force of the law.

(7:2) But Paul does not want to point out only the redemption from the old obligation but also the new obligation to the will of God. He therefore applies that legal maxim to the special case of marital law. Here also death cancels the old law and creates new conditions. The law binds the wife to the husband as long as he lives. On his death the wife is free.

(7:3) The wife's submission to another man during her husband's lifetime is adultery, but she can enter into a new marriage after his death. This example from marital law has a deeper, metaphorical sense for Paul. In the Old Testament, in the prophet Osee for example, the relationship of God and his people is compared to the marriage bond. So also in the New Testament is the relationship of Christ and his Church described as marriage (2 Cor 11:2:

"I betrothed you to one spouse that I might present you a chaste virgin to Christ;" further Eph 5:22–33). In this way the wife in Paul's example signifies from the very beginning the Church.

(7:4) The conclusions are drawn from the legal maxims referred to in 7:1–3. One is that Christians have died to the law, or rather they have been executed to the law with the body of Christ. For Christ has been crucified in their stead, in place of sinners, in order to satisfy the legal claim of sin. (The idea only hinted at here is presented fully in Gal 3:13.) Christians have thus died to the law and are free from it. It has henceforth no more claim to make on them. The other conclusion is: just as the wife becomes free through the death of her first husband and can henceforth belong to another, so Christians are free from the law in order to belong to another, who is Christ.[9]

(7:5) The earlier period under the law and the present period of freedom are contrasted and the thoughts and wording of 6:19–23 are resumed. The earlier period is characterized as "being in the flesh," and the word flesh recurs often in what follows since Paul uses it frequently. He understands the term somewhat differently, however, than we do. In Paul, flesh can simply mean human existence (so 2 Cor 10:3: "We walk in the flesh.") Most often, however, the derogatory sense of the word is accentuated, so that it refers to man as he really and truly conducts his life. This, however, is man given over to sin from his very beginning, man in opposition to God, man for whom all is in vain. In this way everything that man does is fleshly. Even the inventions and creations of the human mind, so understood, are fleshly. The opposite is what stems from the spirit of God and is therefore imperishable. (The Pauline term flesh would thus be misunderstood if one understood it exclusively in terms of the so-called sins of the flesh in the narrowest sense, of unchastity.) The proceeds of that period were sin and death.

(7:6) The antithesis between old and new covenant, law and gospel, is now expressed as that between the old letter and the new spirit (as in 2 Cor 3:6). In the old covenant the service of God was determined by the written ordinances of the law of Moses. They were given to man as severe demands, and since they were not and could not be fulfilled they only increased sin. All this is now done with, outstripped, obsolete. Christians have received the spirit of God. The new service of God is different. The spirit moves man inwardly, it helps him to overcome sin and to serve God in love rather than in fear (cf. 8:15).

(7:7) In 7:7–25, using the first person singular, Paul describes man under the law. Since the time of the Church Fathers exegesis has been occupied with the question of how this "I" is to be understood. Exegesis generally assumes today that Paul is speaking here of unredeemed man in general. Since the reply to this question presupposes a considerable knowledge of the text, the answer will be given in more detail only at the end of the interpretation of Rom 7 (see below, page 116f).

When Paul says in 7:5 that the law arouses sinful passions, the question can finally be asked: do law and sin not ultimately have the same consequences? In the final analysis is not the law itself sin? Perhaps Paul has already been reproached with these conclusions: perhaps by Jews in order to accuse him as a blasphemer; perhaps by Gentiles (i.e. Christian Gentiles) who wanted to despise Israel for that reason.

The phrases with which Paul answers this question are not always easy to understand. Paul seems to be wrestling with the formulation. Yet there are reasons. Sin is an obscure mystery since it always poses anew the question: why is this permitted and why must this be so? Paul's argument becomes more comprehensible if we recognize that he is following the story of the fall in Gen 3. In paradise God gave the commandment: you may not eat of the tree in the middle. This commandment of God was undeniably holy, just and good. But the serpent, i.e. sin, used the commandment, stirred up the longing of man and deceived the first man. Thus sin brought death into the world with the help of the commandment. With this original example of commandment and sin in paradise Paul describes and clears up what commandment and sin are. In that original story the whole history of man is described in advance.

Paul explains and establishes what the law is and defends it. The law was and is one of the great gifts and honors given by God to Israel (9:4). It is holy, good and just (7:12). The law is not sin but it is true that sin uses the law as an aid in order to bring man into its power. It is true that the law goads inordinate longings. When the law prohibits—thou shalt not—then the impulse, previously slumbering, becomes conscious lust. And when the commandment demands—thou shalt—then laziness and malice speak out in opposition. Thus man can say:

without commandment and prohibition I would not have known lust.

(7:8f) Sin uses the law to awaken lust. Through the law sin, which was as if dead, becomes a living force which rules man.

(7:10) God's prohibition in paradise warned: you must not eat of the tree, for the day you eat of it you must die. So it happened. At that time death came into the world as the consequence of sin, and since then sin always brings about death. There arose a fateful reversal. God gave the law to man for protection, order and advancement of life. It was to be a blessing to man. But it become a curse for him and brought him death.

(7:11) The serpent deceived the first human beings in paradise with false promises: no, you shall not die! You will be like God! Sin always deceives man in this way. It buoys him up with false promises of joy, happiness and life, and brings him death.

(7:12) Paul can thus establish: the law is in no way sin. Rather it is holy, that is, it comes from God and belongs to his domain (see under 1:7). It is just as God the Lawgiver is just. It is good for it is a gift of God.

(7:13) Once again Paul takes up the pros and cons. Is it nevertheless not so that God's goodness brings death to man? Does not God as the Lawgiver stand in an ambiguous light? Is he the God of goodness, or a demon who makes a fool of man and thrusts him into perdition? No! It is not God who with the law leads men into disaster but sin— which is at any rate always revealed in all its malice in the end. As long as it was not evident that sin leads finally to death it appeared harmless. But now, since it makes use of the good, misuses it, perverts it into its opposite and leads to death, its real nature comes to light. Now it is disclosed and shown to be "immeasurably sinful."

(7:14) In 7:14–25 Paul further describes the reality of law and sin, life and death with the antithesis of spirit and flesh. Both words must be understood in the sense in which Paul uses them. Spirit, in Paul's sense, is not the spirit or soul of man; thus not the spirit which was given to man in creation and belongs to his nature and elevates him above the animal. Spirit is rather (almost always in Paul and at any rate here) the Spirit of God, the Holy Spirit, thus the power with which God intervenes in the world and in history. For it is God's Spirit who creates life (8:2). Flesh, however, here means (as in 7:5) simply man, who belongs to sin whether he knows and desires it or not, and whose works and life are therefore futile. He supposes that he acts and lives but in reality he has come into the power of death.

The law is "spiritual" for it stems from God's world and contains God's power and life. The calamity is that man's nature is not of the spirit but of the flesh. For this man has decided in favor of sin and is therefore abandoned to it. He is bought as a slave by sin. No slave can ever cancel such a purchase by himself. Nor can man do so. He is no longer his own master.

(7:15 and 7:19)[10] The "I" of man therefore establishes that it becomes in its conduct an inextricable enigma and does not understand its own action. Man no longer finds himself in his own action. The will is certainly to be awakened by the ideal of one's duty, perhaps even to be stirred up to a high blaze, but it is powerless to realize this duty. For that reason the willing "I" hates its own action.

(7:16) By this discord man confirms in the midst of his disobedience that the law is good. His inner "you will!" agrees with the law. He knows that he must fulfill the law. If he nonetheless does evil then he can not excuse himself by saying that the law is evil. Rather he must acknowledge the holy will of God in the law.

(7:17 and 7:20) Man stands finally as such a stranger before his own action that he can no longer recognize and acknowledge it as his own. A strange power has taken up residence within him, a power which rules him and drives him to deeds strange to himself. Man can still differentiate between good and evil but this makes his situation even more desperate, for he himself cannot decide against sin, nor can he free himself from sin. It is not true that man would need only to will it and he would be able to reform and free himself. The judgment has fallen over man. He is a slave sold into sin and it is his master. Paul would not allow, as an excuse for man, that his intention is nonetheless noble and good. For what man is according to his intention is here unimportant. The sense of the commandment is inflexibly the deed. And if man does not keep the commandment he sentences himself to guilt and death.

(7:18) Man knows how his true life would have to be. But he continually fails to live it, since he is flesh. Man's knowledge is no longer a value for him but becomes for him a terrible burden.

(7:21f) The discord in which man lives becomes for him a fetter and restraint from which he cannot free himself on his own. It is, in short, the inevitable law of his life that the inner man joyfully accepts the law of the good and the noble but that the outer man does not follow the inner movement.

(7:23) Around man and in man lie spirit and flesh or, as Paul says here, spirit and the lower self, at war with one another. (Paul uses again the image of war; cf. under 6:13.) But sin has won out and leads the "I" of man away as a captive.

(7:24) Man by himself has no choice. All his efforts do not save him. His good intention does not help him at all. Nothing remains for him in his helplessness but the cry of distress for the Savior from without who is to free him from the life which is in death and directed toward death.[11]

(7:25) The question and call of the most extreme distress receive no answer in the form of a promise. The readers of the epistle know the answer. Paul does not even bother to state it. All know how the cry has been answered. In the Lord Jesus Christ the Church is truly delivered. The gratitude of the redeemed in which all doubt is abolished suddenly declares itself out of powerful agitation and deep violent emotion.

The redemption and the life of the redeemed will be described in Rom 8. Prior to this, however, 7:25 pointedly summarizes once more the result of the sorrowful self-examination. The "I" stands in double servitude. Its reason knows that it is bound to the law of God. But in the fleshly reality it has come into the power of the law of sin.

The question still remains to be answered: to whom do the so severe verses 7:14–25 apply? Who is meant by the "I"? It is certainly evident that Paul is not only speaking of himself but is including himself with men in general under the "I." But then there is the further question: does the redeemed man speak in this way? Paul can hardly utter sentences like 7:17,19,20 about himself as an apostle or, furthermore, about the Christian in general. As an apostle Paul is not aware of any evil deed on his part, so he can assert in 1 Cor 4:4: "True, my conscience makes no charge against me, yet I am not by that fact acquitted." And Paul can certainly not be speaking in 7:17–20 of the redeemed man's servitude under sin and death if he says soon after in 8:2, precisely of the redeemed man: "The law of the spirit which directs my life in Jesus Christ has delivered me from the Law which entices me to sin and leads to death." Thus Paul is speaking in Rom 7 of the "I" of unredeemed man, of Jew and Gentile, who certainly knows the law and agrees with it—be it the law of Moses for the Jew or the law of nature for the Gentile—but remains helplessly abandoned to sin and death.

Paul is writing Rom 7 while looking back from the gospel at the life of natural man under the law. In Rom 8 Paul speaks of the life of redeemed man. But with Rom 7 Paul is also saying to the Christian: every man would have to speak thus of himself if he were left to the law alone, without Christ and without the Spirit of God. Therefore let redeemed man not forget and despise his calling: freedom and grace. Rom 7 also apples to the Christian in another sense, in that he might want to give up election and blessing and believe that he could live on his own capability instead of from the Spirit of God. Then, whether he knew it or not and whether he admitted it or not, he would once more be hopelessly and helplessly living a life that leads to death. The unredeemed state of 7:14–25 is overcome for the believer. But it remains a danger for him which he must always overcome anew.

What Paul says in Rom 7 about the law leads into great breadth and depth. Paul speaks first of all of the Jewish law in the Old Testament which Moses gave. Paul defends the law of the old covenant as God's holy, just and good institution and as his spiritual gift. Paul resists separating forcibly the old and new covenants. In fact it would be disastrous to do so. The book and the law of the old covenant begin on its first pages with the report that the creation of the world and of man was the work of God. "And God saw that it was good." Thus the whole book of the Old Testament and the law which is laid down in it as the book of creation is a witness that the world is God's. It is a reflection of his beauty, grandeur and goodness. It is filled with life, which sprang from the eternal life of God. No one may disparage or despise this creation. Redemption and grace of the new covenant are intended to restore the original creation and to consummate it above and beyond that in the glory of Christ. Old and new covenant, Old and New Testament are together the unity of nature and grace. One may therefore not separate them from one another.

What Paul says in Rom 7 applies not only to Old Testament law but also to moral law and lawfulness in

general. Thus the warning of the apostle applies also to
the Church, her order and her law. The fundamental law
of the Church is God's order, in which the work of salvation is constantly renewed and consummated. To it is
added the law which the Church has given herself to
regulate everyday affairs, just as Paul already did in his
churches according to the principle (1 Cor 14:40): "Only
see that all things are done properly and in good order."
And it is also true of this law that it is just and good. But
good law must not become false legality. The law would
be perverted and misused if it were enacted and enforced
as an external decree and obeyed without the will to serve
love and truth. The will to power can also penetrate the
sanctuary. The law, which is good, would become disastrous
legality if the letter of the law became more important than
the spirit. This would happen if the external ordinance
became more important than the inner content, lip-service
more important than obedience of the heart. The law
would result in false trust in legality if there was more trust
in industrious zeal, or perhaps in pious activity, than in the
freely and abundantly generous love of God. All our activity is human work that remains in the old sphere of
action. Only the creative act of God and his creative
Spirit can liberate and redeem one from that sphere and
enable one to begin anew. All law has sense and justice
only if it paves the way for God and promotes a powerful
awakening.

What Paul says about the impotency of the law applies
also to that other law which man always gives himself
anew in his moral and religious ideas and ideals. In his

striving for knowledge and wisdom man nevertheless always tries again and again to create for himself order and law of his life and of the life of the community which supports him, and to redeem himself—through this law which he gives himself—from meaningless chaos. Who would deny that the mind has thereby created, from antiquity to our own time, magnificent systems of thought? The apostle Paul would say that man with all his effort cannot find the gate out of his helplessness, that he cannot free himself from perdition to sin, and that he cannot open by himself the lost pathway to recovery and salvation. For the apostle says that there is only one santification for man, the sanctification which God wants to give him (3:24,28).

7 THE NEW SPIRIT

8: 1–17

8: 1 So, there is now no longer any condemnation against those who are in Christ Jesus.

2 The law of the spirit which directs my life in Christ Jesus has delivered me from the Law which entices me to sin and leads to death.

3 What was impossible to the Law, in that it was helpless because of corrupt nature, God has effected. By sending his Son in the likeness of sinful flesh and in order to remove sin, he has condemned sin by the incarnation,

4 in order that the requirements of the Law might be fulfilled in us who live no longer according to our lower but according to our higher nature.

5 Now they who live under the control of their lower instincts set their minds on the carnal, but they who live

under the control of spiritual ideals set their minds on the spiritual.

6 Sensual-mindedness leads to death, but spiritual mindedness leads to life and peace.

7 Why? Because sensual-mindedness is hostile to God; it is not subject to the Law of God, nor can it be.

8 The sensual-minded cannot please God.

9 You, however, are not sensual but spiritual, if the Spirit of God really dwells in you, whereas no one who is deprived of the Spirit of Christ belongs to Christ.

10 But if Christ is in you, the body, it is true, is destined to death because of sin, but the spirit has life because of its holiness.

11 And if the Spirit of him who raised Jesus from the dead dwells in you, then he who raised Christ Jesus from the dead will also bring to life your mortal bodies because of his Spirit who dwells in you.

12 Therefore, brothers, you are under no obligation to your lower nature to live according to its promptings.

13 If you live according to the flesh you will die; but if by the spirit you put to death the deeds prompted by the flesh, you will live.

14 Whoever are led by the Spirit of God, they are the sons of God.

15 Now you have not received a spirit of bondage so that you are again in fear, but you have received a spirit of adoption as sons, in virtue of which we cry, "Abba! Father!"

16 The Spirit himself joins his testimony to that of our spirit that we are children of God.

17 But if we are children, we are heirs also: heirs indeed of God and joint heirs with Christ, since we suffer with him that we may also be glorified with him.

No chapter of the Epistle to the Romans has been so important to the Church Fathers as Rom 8. This chapter is quoted by them far more than all others, and no other chapter do they interpret so carefully and so penetratingly as this one. The Fathers recognized here the center of the Epistle to the Romans. This is perhaps an essential difference between the early Church's interpretation of the epistle and that of the Reformation (whose great significance for its historically effective interpretation of the epistle no one will deny). Of greatest importance for the Reformation is what the epistle says of law and sin, of faith and assurance of justification. Concerning this the epistle discloses to man his desperate state. He is to comfort himself in the confidence of forgiveness and grace. Beyond this and important above all to the Fathers is what the epistle reveals of the new life in the Spirit as an already present certainty. In this interpretation the epistle is the witness to God's love, already and permanently given, and to the Christian who, through the gift of the Spirit, is already in possession of the unutterable riches of the redemption.

(8:1) A complete change has come about. Previously the "I" even with all its good intentions stood hopelessly under the death sentence toward which it inescapably hastened. But now the believer, in that he belongs to those who are in Christ, stands under acquittal.

(8:2) Old and new order come face to face. Previously sin and death passed for the law since man stood under their mastery, forced to do what he did not want to do. That was the severe Old Testament law. But now a new order of the Spirit and of life has canceled and overcome the old. Naturally, redemption and salvation also have their order. The Spirit is not vague, aimless fanaticism, not mere distant idea and impotent ideal, but a Spirit operative in order and law. Law and freedom are not opposites. Rather the Spirit creates freedom. And he brings life—both the present, new, meaningful life and the life to come at the end of time. The Spirit is given in the Christ Jesus. This statement testifies anew that the Spirit is not fanaticism. He is given through Christ—thus wherever the disciple hears the word of the Lord and follows his passion and salvation. And he is given in Christ—thus wherever communion with him really exists, i.e. in the Church. For those who are in Christ make up his Church. Only here and only thus is freedom. Otherwise man is always in his own imprisonment.

(8:3) Old and new age are compared with one another. The law also stood and stands against sin, had nothing to do with it and desired the freedom of man from sin. Yet sin ruled all the same. The law did condemn sin but it was not able to divest it of its power and overcome it. For because of his fleshly nature man was not able to fulfill the law. For that reason sin prevailed. Since the law was not able to pave the way out of sin God chose another way. He sent his Son "in the likeness of sinful flesh." Paul's carefully considered formulation expresses the reality of the incarnation and the absolute humanity of Christ. He appeared in the flesh, as a human being like us. He was wholly man, with human knowledge and volition. His sinlessness was not only because of his divine nature but was also accomplished by him in his human obedience. Through this obedience sin was weakened and overcome. Paul says, to be sure, that Christ appeared in the likeness of sinful flesh, but he does not say that he lived in sinful flesh. Such a statement would be impossible for the apostle. The corporeality of Christ is a true corporeality but it is not a corporeality subjugated to sin. There is an essential difference between Christ and man. He entered into the human race, took its sin upon himself, yet remained without sin (2 Cor 5:21: "For our sakes God made sin of him who knew no sin, so that in him we might become God's holiness"). Thus God now sent his Son for the sake of sin, to condemn and overcome sin in the flesh. With these words Paul is pointing toward the cross. Christ died the death which sinners had deserved. Now sin has been satisfied. The demanding justice of God has also been satisfied.

(8:4) Christ's work of salvation brings not only the condemnation of sin but also the fulfillment of the law. To be sure, all superficial legality is abolished. But the true law is still God's word and order and they must endure and be fulfilled. Jesus demands it (Mt 5:17) and so does Paul. But it is no longer a question of a multitude of commandments which surely no one can fulfill; it is rather a simple and comprehensive sanctification according to divine will, a sanctification which consists in the faith which finds its expression in love. This sanctification can now be realized by those to whom is given the Spirit, who overcomes the flesh. All Christians are in this position and have this potentiality. For it is stated again in Rom 8 that the Spirit is given to all Christians. The gift of the Spirit constitutes the Christians. Without it they wouldn't be Christians at all (8:9). All Christians are therefore "religious" ("spiritual"). The custom that priests and monks, in contrast to laymen, call themselves religious only came into use in the fourth century, when the emperor Constantine had raised Christianity to the state religion and the masses streamed in to the Church. Those who now called themselves religious wanted to assert thereby that they took Paul and the New Testament seriously, as the masses were perhaps not willing or able to do. Yet all Christians must not forget that they all have the honor and the duty to be "religious."

(8:5) In 8:5–11, the life of the flesh and the life in the spirit are contrasted; 8:6–8 deals mainly with the flesh, 8:9–11 mainly with the spirit. Conduct according to the flesh stems naturally from existence according to the flesh. Conduct according to the spirit is only possible for he who is in the Spirit. The Spirit which Paul refers to here is not the spirit of man but the Spirit of God (see under 7:14). The life of the Spirit therefore stems not simply from the good intentions of man; rather existence according to the Spirit is first necessary. This, however, is God's act of salvation to man.

(8:6) Therefore death and life are not two aims in life which man could choose as he wished. Rather whatever the flesh—that is, natural man—seeks, thinks and works at on his own is death. Of course the endeavors of natural man strive for an intensification of life in every way: by gaining property and power, by fulfilling everyday and elevated love, by developing and working with the mind, and also by practicing and accomplishing virtue. Yet the apostle can only say that everything that man undertakes on his own is in vain because it is ephemeral and fallen into the power of death. Only the God-given power of the Spirit will find life. Only thus can redemption from death and obtainment of life come about: only thus can the peace which is salvation (see under 1:7) be obtained.

(8:7f) Just as natural man, whether he knows it or not, is always progressing toward death, so also does he always live as the adversary of God. He always opposes God and his law for the aim of the flesh is always rebellion. For the wishes and desires of man, who from Adam on is in his basic attitude far from God and hostile to him, are always directed toward evil. They cannot follow the will of God for they would then cease to be what they are. Man can therefore not reform himself, and because of this he can never please God. Only God himself was and is able to accomplish a change.

(8:9) This change has now been consummated in the act of God and in the gift of the Spirit. Christians are no longer in the flesh, i.e. no longer in the general sinful existence. Paul bears witness to the great new reality. He knows that Christians can still commit sin. All his epistles speak of the fact that there are errors and sins in the Church. In the Epistle to the Romans too there are urgent warnings not to relax in the struggle with evil and to help the Spirit to victory. But it is established that what has taken place is decisive because God has done it. The Church and all Christians have experienced God's Spirit. This took place in concrete reality through faith and baptism (1 Cor 12:13: "By a single spirit all of us were introduced into the one body through baptism"). Those who endure in the faith are henceforth capable of living from the Spirit.

(8:10) The new reality means that what Christ accomplished for Christians belongs to them. In his death he has condemned sin, deprived it of its power and executed it. Thus the body also, insofar as it belonged to sin, is executed. Paul does not despise the body.[12] The body as such is not executed, but the body, i.e. the life, which belonged to sin. Now the body is ennobled in that it is redeemed and sanctified. Man, however, is now able to truly live out of the Spirit and holiness of God which are given to him. Only a life which belongs to holiness and to the Spirit is true life.

(8:11) This life will in the future unfold itself in its entire fullness and will take hold of the body. Not only is the soul saved but the Spirit vouches for complete regeneration. The body is still mortal and its mortality is and remains the sign of the fall and of sin. But now the body of Christ has been killed for the sake of sin, and with it the body of the Christian. He who raised the body of Christ from the dead will also raise the Christians. This will come about through the Spirit of God, in whom God accomplishes his works in the world. God has now wrought a new creation for he raised Jesus from the dead as "the first fruits of those that have fallen asleep in death" (1 Cor 15:20). But this is only the beginning of the redemption. The same God who raised Christ consummates his work in that he redeems through his Spirit the mortality of man in life. Paul does not speak of the philosophical immortality innate to man as an intellectual being. The life which he proclaims is not the natural dowry of man but rather God's act of salvation on man. It has a glory which philosophy cannot suspect. Not only are dead bodies restored to life. Much more than that! Nothing that man does in faith, no good thought, no attempted act of love is vain and futile, nothing is lost. Everything is secure in God and is kept in store with him until the great Easter Day which he will bring.

(8:12) Paul speaks forcefully of the act of God. Then follow the first admonitions (8:12–17). The teaching on baptism (6:1–10) was likewise followed by the exhortation to realize one's baptism (6:12–23). Paul has declared: you live in the spirit! Now follows the exhortation: live according to the spirit! The flesh is dead! So kill the flesh! The life of the Christian is decided by God's act of redemption. And this decisiveness places him in the position of decision between the flesh and the Spirit. Naturally the Christian is called to freedom and redeemed. But this freedom is not freedom for sin. It is indebtedness to God and thereby, to be sure, true freedom for the first time.

(8:13) The decision before which the Christian stands has consequences of extreme conclusiveness. He decides between death and life. The life of the flesh obtains death, the life of the Spirit gains life.

(8:14) The Spirit leads to the sonship of God. As the Spirit of God he produces in man a uniformity and unanimity with God. He who lets himself be led by the Spirit thinks God's thoughts and lets his life be determined by the will of God. He becomes uniform with God, as a son with the father. But sons are heirs (8:17) and if God is life God's sons will also possess it.

(8:15) What being a son means and includes becomes clear from its opposite: being a slave. Until now, of course, slavery prevailed, inasmuch as the law prevailed, for the law generated only sin and with it fear of punishment. The

era of the law is over; the Christian is no longer a slave but
the son of God. The proof is prayer, for in prayer the word
Father, as an address to God, streams from the heart of the
Christian.[13] Thus he who prays in this manner is a son.

(8:16) He who prays always remains, however, only a
creature, a sinner before the great and holy God. If man
wanted to call God Father merely on his own it would
certainly be an error, even impudence, if on his own he
believed that God and he were as close to one another as
this address declares. But Paul knows and the Christian
knows that the believer does not so speak on his own. He
experiences as certain that it is truly God's Spirit in man
which, together with our own spirit, calls Father. And it
is not merely the spirit of the individual but rather the
Spirit who fills the whole Church who from many hearts
united calls Father. The common prayer of the Church
demonstrates her common certainty of adoption before God.
This comprehensive community cannot be mistaken.

(8:17) Just as will the children of every father, so too
will the children of God have a share in the blessings of
their Father. These blessings are God's eternal salvation.
According to filial rights the children will "inherit" these
blessings. The New Testament often uses the word inheritance in this sense. It speaks of the inheritance of the kingdom of God (Mt 25:34), of eternal life (Mk 10:17), of
salvation (Hebr 1:14), of the blessing (1 Pet 3:9). The
inheritance is always a gift, never earnings. Thus the New
Testament wants to express with this word that God's gift
is not owed. The security, however, that we will attain this
inheritance is Christ, the one Son. He abides already in

community with the Father for he has already received the glorious inheritance. He will unite his brothers with himself. But Christ has attained the inheritance by his suffering of death. Thus the way of his disciples can only lead through the passion.

8   THE CERTAINTY
OF THE CONSUMMATION

8:18–39

8:18 Why, I count the sufferings of the present time as not worthy to be compared with the glory to come that will be revealed shining upon us.

19 All creation awaits with eager longing the manifestation of the sons of God.

20 For creation was made subject to vanity not by its own choice but by the will of him who made it subject,

21 yet with the hope that creation itself would be delivered from its slavery to corruption, to enjoy the freedom which comes with the glory of the children of God.

22 For we know that all creation groans and travails in pain until now.

23 And not only that, but we ourselves who have the Holy Spirit as first fruits—we ourselves groan within ourselves, waiting for the adoption as sons, the redemption of the body.

24 As yet, our salvation is only a matter of hope. Now there is no hope when the object which had been hoped for is seen. How can a man hope really for what he sees?

25 But if we hope for what we do not see, we wait for it with patience.

26 In the same way the Spirit also helps our weakness. For we do not know what we should pray for as we ought, but

the Spirit himself pleads for us with unutterable sighs.

27 And he who searches the hearts knows what the Spirit desires and that he in accord with God's designs pleads for the saints.

28 Now we know that in all things which are for their good, God works together with those who love him, who according to his purpose are called;

29 for those whom he has foreknown he has also predestined to be conformed to the image of his Son, so that this Son should be the first-born among many brothers.

30 Those whom he has predestined, he has called; and those whom he has called, he has sanctified, and those whom he has sanctified, he has glorified.

31 What then shall we conclude after that? If God is for us, who is against us?

32 He who has not spared even his own Son but has delivered him for us all, how can he fail to grant us all other blessings with him?

33 Who shall make accusation against the elect of God? It is God who sanctifies!

34 Who shall condemn? It is Christ Jesus who died, yes, and who rose again, who is at the right hand of God, who also intercedes for us!

35 Who shall separate us from Christ's love for us? Shall tribulation, or distress, or persecution, or hunger, or nakedness, or danger, or the sword?

36 Even as it is written,
"For your sake we are put to death all the day long, we are regarded as sheep for the slaughter" (Ps 43:23).

37 But in all those things we are more than victorious through him who has loved us.

38 I am sure that neither death, nor life, nor angels, nor principalities, nor things present, nor things to come, nor powers,

39 nor height, nor depth, nor any other creature can separate us from God's love for us, which is in Christ Jesus our Lord.

Paul sees reality as it is, full of distress. He knows the Church is not yet redeemed and the world is not yet healed. But with the same sobriety he also knows what the salvation already accomplished means in this age: we are saved in anticipation of the future (8:24). In the midst of this distress faith and hope have their confidence, for they know that the merciful God will consummate all the longing of the world. This longing is revealed in the groan for consummation which cries out from irrational creation (8:19–22); in the groan for fulfillment which still moves even the sons (8:23–25); and finally in the groan of the Holy Spirit who represents men's hearts before God (8:26).

(8:18) In face of the present one must hold to the future and know that all distress does not weigh nearly as heavily as the glory that is to come. If it is weighed, however, it has its limits for it was God who measured its length and its weight. The glory awaits the revelation to us. Whatever waits for revelation is already present, although still invisible. Redeemed man is still a mystery. There is something about him still hidden from sight. Still veiled, it is now only attainable in faith.

(8:19) Paul perceives longing and anxiety as the basic manifestations of all created life. But he is able to interpret the cause, significance and claim of this longing. All creatures are waiting for the hitherto hidden glory of the sons of God to be revealed to the world. For this revelation will bring about the liberation of creation for glory.

What Paul says becomes more comprehensible if we perceive to what extent it participates in a long and profound tradition.[14] Thus the prophet Isaia already announces God's promise (65:17): "Lo, I am about to create new heavens and a new earth." In the New Testament the Apocalypse of John (21:1–4) depicts with marvelous colors the new heaven, and the new earth which is free of sickness, sorrow and death.[15]

(8:20) Creation is waiting to be redeemed with man for it was, through no fault of its own, condemned to death along with man. Paul recalls the story of creation. Because of the sin of the first human beings the earth was also cursed (Gen 3:17f: "Cursed be the ground because of you; Thorns and thistles shall it bring forth to you"). Yet from the very beginning God gave in his promises hope for the abrogation of this state of affairs and future salvation.

(8:21) Just as creation is bound with man to corruption so also is it bound with him to salvation, and will be freed with him from transiency and death. Death is not to cease only for man, thus not only in one place. Therefore nature will also be freed with men from the power of death. Yet not only this; in addition it is to attain the glory of the children of God.

(8:22) We still hear with Paul the chorus of groans from the tormented world. But it is not only a cry from the tragic agony of despair. It is the travail of the world lying in labor. God does not let innocent nature cry out in vain. The present time of distress surely points toward the future liberation.

Man and world stand for Paul in an intimate community of destiny. Man is not redeemed out of the world but with it. Redemption does not mean that man is carried off into a hereafter where he may look down on the world abandoned to its fate. Man lives closely bound to the world in and by his body for he is a part of it. And God, the one Creator of the whole world, will renew and consummate it as the one world. It is in man, however, that creation has its center and its meaning. "The history of mankind with God is the pulsating heart of the whole world."

(8:23) No way less than the rest of creation, the sons of God themselves await the revelation of salvation and groan in their longing for it. Up to now they have not received the whole reality of their sonship, but have been given only a portion in advance. This advance gift is the Spirit who is, as it were, the first installment on all the riches which God will give. He is only a partial gift and for this reason there is still distress; the body is still in the power of death. Yet the partial gift contains the certainty that the whole abundance will one day be given. The sons groan in this intermediary state for the consummation. But precisely the tension between the visible reality and the hidden state of redemption is the reason for certainty, for it will not remain a partial gift. The complete gift of sonship must certainly follow. This complete salvation, after the present gift of the Spirit, will be the redemption of the body, i.e. the new, transfigured corporeality. For this body, still given over to death, certainly remains the most impressive sign of the redemption which has not yet taken place but which is only awaited and anticipated.

(8:24) But despite all present distress it holds true that the believers are rescued and safe in their hope. That does not mean that they hope one day to be saved; rather they are saved in that they were placed in anticipation of the future by God's act of salvation. It is true that hope is not yet possession and that faith hopes for blessings which it has not yet seen. But that is no lessening of hope; rather it signifies its grandeur. Hope anticipates blessings which exceed everything known on earth. Hope must not base itself on something visible for everything visible is transient and perishable. Only the invisible is eternal (so also in 2 Cor 4:18: "We direct our gaze not at what is seen but at what is unseen. What we see is temporary, but what we do not see endures forever").

(8:25) The Church waits patiently in the certainty of consummation. This patience distinguishes certain from fantastic hope: the one is capable of waiting in patience whereas the other is impatient, for it is based only on uncertainty and makes do with errors. For this reason it does not have the strength to persevere under the severity of reality.

(8:26) Paul hears the groaning from a still deeper realm. Illusion would still be possible; if we heard only the groans of creation, only the crying out of human hearts, what would guarantee that an answer would follow? Would the cry have to find help merely because it shouts so loudly? Does every cry find a favorable hearing? But now there is yet another groan of an entirely different nature which has within itself the certainty of being heard. The Spirit who is given to us, who stems from that other world to which all groaning is directed, the Spirit takes up our groan and intercedes for us before the throne of God. This groan will surely find a favorable hearing. This groan of the Spirit expresses itself in the prayer of the Church. Our own merely personal prayer would not be able to have such great confidence. For we do not know what we should pray and how it is proper.[16] The main thing would be to say what is fitting, i.e. what corresponds to God's holiness, power and love. But man can never build the bridge from his world into the wholly different world of God. Is man's prayer thus a senseless undertaking which never reaches its goal? This is not the case because the prayer of faith is a mysterious phenomenon between God and man. For God takes man's incapacity upon himself. The Spirit of God apprehends our prayer and intercedes for it before the throne of God. He purifies it so that our prayer becomes fitting worship and supplication. He translates man's words into the language of the divine world. It is a language which man can neither understand nor speak on his own. It is for him an unutterable groan of which only the Spirit is capable. This prayer brings before God not foolish human wishes but the true and longing supplication which we ourselves do not know. God himself shares through his Spirit the distress of creation. The divine Spirit himself, given to man, groans for liberation. This prayer will surely be granted.

(8:27) For God, who understands everything and exhausts everything which lies at the bottom of our hearts, understands yet more fully the prayer of the Spirit, of his Spirit. He understands that the Spirit intercedes for the saints, i.e. the believers (1:7), for in them the Holy Spirit breathes.

(8:28) From all sides the groan presses forward to God. So many requests will not remain unanswered. This is guaranteed by one last pledge, the strongest of all, namely,

God's will to salvation. It includes everyone who loves God.[17] Those who love God, however, are those who have first been loved by him, for they are also "those whom he has called." And according to 5:5, to love God means to respond to the love of God, who has loved first. Therefore everything must certainly help to secure the good of those who love God for they are the loved ones of God. That everything contributes to their good does not mean, however, that things go better for the Christian than for others during this earthly life. But since they have been called their final salvation is certain.

(8:29f) The exegesis of the Church Fathers has called the series of words in 8:29f "the golden chain." Just as one word follows from and is linked to the other so are God's works of salvation linked to one another. Thus God's will stirs man according to a fixed plan and leads him to the final goal. Both the beginning ("he has foreknown them") and the end ("he has glorified them") of the chain hang from God's eternity. Thus election proceeds from and leads back to eternity. The first act is God's foreknowledge of man. It is not (as it was occasionally understood in the history of exegesis) a divine foreknowledge of future virtue and future merits, the reward for which God has already decided. If this was true God would decide and choose as men do because it is worthwhile. Then God would be dependent on man and everything would depend on the latter's performance. Justification would then no longer be summons of the sinner and creative work of God, but the rewarding of virtuous man. God's love, however, is much greater and much more powerful. God's choice is his free act, which breaks through everything, even sin. God does not find those who are to be chosen, he creates them. When God knows man it is not an impartial, neutral taking note of something but creative grace and love (thus Jer 15: "Before I formed you in the womb I knew you"). Those who are foreknown are predestined to be molded in the image of the Son of God who now lives in divine majesty. This glory is also prepared for the Christian who now possesses the preliminary gift of the Spirit. One day they are to receive their full stature. Christ is therefore the first-born among many brothers. This brotherhood does not invalidate the uniqueness of Christ; he remains the First. But the image of the Son is God's plan for mankind and all men are to be molded in the image of the Son of God. Christ is the goal and the sense of history. He is what man in truth is and should become. (The same thing is said in 5:4 when Christ is called the new Adam.)

(8:30) The eternal divine acts of the election and the predestination enter into history in the summoning and sanctification of man and they lead back to eternity in the glorification. Paul is able to say that God already *has* glorified. He can be so sure of this last act that he can speak of it as something that has already occurred. The chain of Paul's words states emphatically that all of God's acts are indestructibly linked together. One link of the chain interlocks securely into the next. No power can step in between; no power, that is, except man himself, who can tear the chain to pieces.

(8:31) Paul has expressed with confident certainty the Church's great self-assurance that it is God's one chosen and beloved community. Yet this Church is perhaps a penniless little band of men—it was so, at least, in that time and in that world. The Christians had perhaps to defend themselves against derision and superior strength from without. And they fought with doubt in their hearts that they could withstand the oppression. But opposing all doubts Paul draws the conclusion: God declares himself and stands by us! With that the decision is made.

Meanwhile God is with us—is this not the battle-cry with which all sides go to war whenever it is a question of winning divine consecration for human goals and wishes? God is for us! This can be true not when man asserts it on his own, even though he so wishes it, but only when God gives him the obvious right to do so.

(8:32) The irrefutable proof that God is for us is that he gave to us what was dearest to him, his Son. It is such an overwhelmingly great gift that those who have thus been favored may now expect all other good gifts from God.

(8:33) Paul sees the Christians as if before the judgment. On all sides stand those who have come to accuse and condemn them. Yet will anyone dare complain about God's elect, on whom he has already decided?

(8:34) They may be guilty sinners worthy of every punishment, yet no condemnation can ensue. For Christ has already taken all condemnation upon himself in his death. And yet more! He lives and sits at the right hand of God[18] and intercedes with him for his own against all condemnation. He is their advocate in the judgment. (Likewise in 1 Jn 2:1: "My little children, I write this letter to keep you from sin. Yet if anyone should commit a sin, we have an advocate with the Father, Jesus Christ, the Holy one.")

(8:35) It is thus the safeguard and the love of Christ which protect us and on which we depend. Therefore the apostle poses the anxious question: can anything separate us from Christ? Perhaps distress, want or oppression? It is the question, for Christians as for the world, of how it is possible that they who are the redeemed must nevertheless —and perhaps all the more—suffer severe distress. The Christian like the apostle always carries the palpable death of Christ around with him and is daily given up to death (2 Cor 4:11f). Paul takes this question seriously and does not simply pass rapturously over reality. On his missionary journeys he has himself frequently known all the difficulties which he enumerates—he lists the almost superhuman troubles of these journeys in 2 Cor 11:23–33. He names last of all the sword, which can only be the executioner's sword. The danger of civil persecution is already mounting although the peaceful relations presupposed in 13:1–7 still endure for a short period. Paul's words are deeply moving for in truth he predicts his own fate. He already sees the sword bared above his head—the sword which will strike him a few years later on the road to Ostia.

(8:36) Even the Pauline Church herself experiences Ps 43:23. Originally this psalm was the nation's prayer of lamentation in the bitter distress of a lost war. Evidence from rabbinical exegesis of the Psalms from that period shows us that Israel already understood Ps 43:23 of its martyrs. (Paul thus follows—as he often does—the biblical exegesis which was practiced in his time and which he had learned in the rabbinical school.) Thus the Church is the

Israel on which the psalm is henceforth fulfilled. Just as the old community of God was persecuted and was not to live on the earth, so now will the new community of God, the Church, also suffer. Of course she knows that she is persecuted for the sake of God and Christ but this does not make the distress easier to bear, and perhaps makes it even harder. Does it not seem that God is neither willing nor able to protect his Church? Does not her external decline appear at least to the world as though her life was of no more value than that of sacrificial animals? Paul does not minimize the distresses. He does not pretend that the loneliness of prisons and the sharpness of the sword is bliss.

(8:37) What remains in all this? Our faith perhaps, the faith of the Church, our bravery, our love? All that would not endure. The faithful can only hold out through him who has loved and loves sinners. This love does not guard one against difficulties but preserves one in them. Paul speaks exuberantly; it does not satisfy him to say: we are victorious! Rather he says: in all those things we are more than victorious!

(8:38) This certainty must prevail against powerful forces. Once more Paul enumerates the powers which threaten to force their way between God and the faith. He enumerates them as natural, historical dangers and as sinister, demonic powers. Paul first names death, after having just spoken of the sword. The word life, which appears as its opposite, is not merely a filler word. Life can also be an impious power, that biological predominance whose spell lets everything else be forgotten or whose demands stifle everything intellectual. But "our wrestling is not against weak human nature, but against the Principalities and the Powers, against those that rule the world of darkness, the wicked spirits that belong to an order higher than ours" (Eph 6:12).

(8:39) According to the conceptions of that period these powers inhabit and fill up the super-terrestrial expanses of the atmosphere and the expanses of the satanic underworld. Yet any assault is from the outset and in the end impotent and futile for they are only created powers. What can they do against the power which stands opposed to them, the eternal love of God? And it is always open to us in Jesus Christ.

FOOTNOTES TO CHAPTER III

[1] It is well known that Martin Luther translated thus, and stressed "by faith alone." But he was not the first by far to understand in this way; the Church Fathers so interpreted and completed the passage before him, starting with the Roman Bishop Clemens (I Clemens 32:4) at the end of the first century. In the same sense Origen explains (Migne, *Patrologia Graeca* 14:952–954) that the works, for which boasting is excluded, are not only the Jewish works of the law but also chastity, wisdom and justice. "All boasting about works is excluded, for it does not have the humility of Christ's cross."

[2] Paul seems to be using ancient Jewish liturgical formulas in these titles he confers on God. In the *Schemoneh 'Esreh*, which goes back to New Testament times and is used to this day in the service of the synagogue, it states: "May thou be praised, Yahweh, who bringest the dead to life." In another text (Syrian Apocalypse of Baruch 48:8) stands: "With a word thou callest into life what does not exist."

[3] In verses 5:6–10 Paul does not seem to find the correct formulations immediately. He begins, interrupts and corrects himself, until his thought, in 5:8 and 5:10, finds satisfactory expression. One sees here for once how Paul shapes and forms thoughts and words. Paul dictated his epistles, as a direct address to the recipients, to a scribe (who adds a greeting himself in 16:22), without afterward smoothing over all the rough spots in the lively conversation. But at the same time the fussiness of the language here must be not only awkwardness but an indication and expression of something unheard of and incomprehensible.

[4] The New Testament often uses the image of the saints reigning

royally with God; thus Lk 22:30, 1 Cor 6:2; Apoc 20:4: "I saw thrones and men seated on them."

5 According to Catholic teaching children who die in a state of original sin, but without personal sin, do not experience the same punishment as personally guilty sinners.

6 It should be noted that the above sentence, as occasionally happens, is unjustly imputed to Martin Luther. At most he understood it as a joke.

7 As in 6:13 the history of man and of the world in which he lives is described as a struggle between good and evil in numerous texts of the New Testament, and fully in Eph 6:10–20. It occurs similarly in nonbiblical texts, especially graphically in the text recently discovered in Qumran, "War of the Sons of Light with the Sons of Darkness."

8 Impurity and lawlessness, according to the judgment of the Jews, is the life of the Gentile. He is impure since he does not know the Jewish regulations of purity (concerning food, the dead, sexuality). He is lawless since he does not keep the written law of Moses.

9 The examples and metaphors which Paul fashions are often laboriously constructed and inconsistent in details; so also, certainly, 7:1–4. They differ in this respect from the parables of Jesus which because of their clarity and truth have imprinted themselves unforgettably in the memory of mankind. But Jesus speaks as the divinely simple teacher, Paul as the brainracking, deductive theologian.

10 Paul's laborious struggle with these thoughts leads him to repetitions: 7:15b corresponds to 7:19, 7:17 corresponds to 7:20.

11 Paul does not desire that the soul should be freed from the perishable body. Plato would have been able to pray in this way, but Paul cannot do so. Paul, with the entire Bible, cannot imagine or desire the existence of the bodiless, "naked" soul (2 Cor 5:3f). Rather Paul anticipates the deliverance of the entire man from the existence leading to death.

12 Paul is a Jew and Jewry is never hostile to the body. Rather it expects, and Paul with it, the resurrection of the body in glory. Later Greek civilization, at most, is hostile to the body.

13 The prayer in which the Christian calls God Father is the Our

Father. As the prayer which Jesus himself had taught to the disciples it is as precious and holy to Paul and his Church as it is to the Church today. The Church does not merely take up in this prayer a word from the mouth of Jesus. Rather faith always lives confidently in that relationship to God which Jesus taught in this prayer, that is, in the relationship of the child before his father.

[14] The Bible of the Old and New Testaments does not anticipate the destruction of the world, but rather a new world: so also, God is never the God of destruction and death, but always of salvation and life.

[15] It becomes clear that Paul takes up Jewish ideas of his time if one compares the rabbinical text from practically the same period: "Although things had been created in their fullness, they were corrupted, after the first man had sinned; and they will not revert to their order until the Messiah comes."

[16] This sentence of Paul is explained from Jesus' words on prayer. Jesus condemns the noisily ostentatious prayer of the often enough splendid celebrations of the heathen cults (Mt 6:7). But he likewise condemns the masterly-pious prayer of the zealous Pharisees both in the synagogue and in public (Mt 6:5). Only the publican prays genuinely for it is he who knows that he cannot pray (Lk 18:10–14).

[17] This love "is separated from everything, even from all religious eros, by the flashing sword of death and of eternity, which announces that here the new man, who neither woos nor lets himself be wooed, stands before God, with Whom, unlike Baal and his kind, no courtship of any kind is to be carried on" (Karl Barth).

[18] Verse 8:34 arranges in a series: he died, rose again and sits at the right hand of God. In many passages of the New Testament, as in this one, traces of the Apostles' Creed, already developing, are found; cf. especially 1 Cor 15:3f. The Apostles' Creed thus bears its name with reason inasmuch as it goes back to the times of the apostolic Church in important phrases.

IV THE HISTORY OF ISRAEL
AND THE HISTORY OF SALVATION

9:1—11:36

In the first large section of the epistle (1:18–8:39) Paul has presented the gospel of God's justification. He concluded (8:25–39) by exalting about the salvation for everyone whom God has chosen and called. Without transition, exaltation is followed in rapid succession by the grievous question, the moving lamentation about Israel. How does it stand with Israel, the people of the revelation and the promise, chosen by God? Paul always said: first the Jew, then the Gentile (1:16; 2:9; 3:9). Has the people of salvation history become the people abandoned by God? Must not Israel's unbelief be a severe hindrance for the credibility and the efficacy of missionary preaching? These are questions which distress Paul both as a Jew deeply bound to his people and as a messenger of the word of God. The question is today just as difficult for the whole Church in the presence of the world. Israel herself, out of which came forth the Savior proclaimed in the Church, refused him. The apostle wrestles with these questions in Rom 9–11. His insights and his interpretations of history are of lasting importance for the Church.

1   ISRAEL'S ELECTION

9: 1–33

9: 1 I speak the truth in Christ, I do not lie, my conscience bears me witness in the Holy Spirit,

2 that I have great sadness and continual sorrow in my heart.

3 For I could wish to be cut off myself from Christ for the sake of my brothers, my kinsmen according to the flesh.

4 They are Israelites. Theirs is the adoption as sons, theirs the glory, the covenants, the legislation, the worship, and the promises.

5 The patriarchs are theirs, and from them has been derived the human nature of Christ, who exalted above all things, is God blessed forever. Amen.

6 It is not that the word of God has failed. They are not all Israelites who are sprung from Israel;

7 nor, because they are the descendants of Abraham, are they all his children; but

"Through Isaac shall your posterity bear your name" (Gen 21:12).

8 That is to say, not they are sons of God who are the children by natural descent, but it is the children designated by the promise who are reckoned as descendants.

9 Here are the terms of the promise: "About this time I will come and Sara shall have a son" (Gen 18:10).

10 And not only she, but Rebecca too conceived by one man, Isaac our father.

11 Why, before the children had been born, or had done aught of good or evil, in order that God's selective purpose might stand,

12 depending not on deeds, but on him who calls, it was said to her, "The elder shall serve the younger" (Gen 25:23).

13 So it is written, "Jacob I have loved, but Esau I have hated" (Mal 1:2f).

14 What then shall we say? Is there injustice in God? By no means!

15 Does he not say to Moses, "I shall have mercy on whom I have mercy, and I will show pity to whom I show pity"? (Ex 33:19).

16 So then, there is no question of him who wills or of him who runs, but of God showing mercy.

17 For example the Scripture says to the Pharao, "For this very purpose I have raised you up, that I may show my power, and that my name may be proclaimed in all the earth" (Ex 9:16).

18 Therefore he has mercy on whom he pleases, and he hardens whom he pleases.

19 Then you will ask me: "Why does God still find fault? Does anyone resist his will?"

20 Of course not, O man, but who are you to answer back to God? Does the object molded say to him who molded it: "Why have you made me thus?" (Is 29:16; 45:9)

21 Or is not the potter master of the clay, free to make from the same material one vessel for honorable, another for dishonorable use?

22 If God who intends to show his wrath and make his power known, endured long and patiently those who deserved his wrath and were ripe for destruction, what can be said against that?

23 He intends thus to show the wealth of his glory on those who are objects of his mercy, whom beforehand he has prepared for that glory.

24 We whom he has called, Jews and Gentiles alike, are the objects of that mercy.

25 So also he says in Osee:
    "A people not mine I will call my people,
        and her who was not beloved, beloved, (Os 2:25)

26   And it shall be in the place where it was said to them:
        you are not my people;

there they shall be called sons of the living God
(Os 2:1).

27 Isaias cries out concerning Israel:
"Though the number of the children of Israel
be as the sands of the sea,
the remnant shall be saved.
28   Surely the Lord will accomplish his word,
cutting it short in his justice" (Is 10:22f).
29 And as Isaias foretold:
"Unless the Lord of Hosts had left us some descendants,
we should have become as Sodom
and should have been like Gomorrah" (Is 1:9).
30 What then are we to say? That the Gentiles who were not
pursuing holiness have secured holiness, the holiness that
comes of faith,
31 while Israel, though pursuing a law leading to holiness,
have not attained to holiness.
32 Why? Because they sought it not from faith but from
deeds. They stumbled at the stumbling stone,
33 as it is written,
"See, I lay in Sion a stumbling stone and rock to
trip over;
But no one who believes in him shall be disappointed" (Is 8:14; 28:16).

Paul looks over the history of Israel, from the begin-
nings to the present, and on until the end of time.
The history of the blessing of Israel reveals to him the nature of God, which is divinely free mercy. Thus does God
deal with Israel. Accordingly Paul is able to interpret
Israel's history.

(9:1) Solemnly and passionately, his words ever more in-
tensive, Paul asserts the truth of what he is about to say. He
appeals to his community with Christ, in which a lie is not

possible, and to his conscience, enlightened by the Spirit of God.

(9:2) The apostle is unceasingly filled with pain and sorrow for the fate of his people. He is not moved merely by an emotional outbreak; rather this is the one lasting, great and grievous sorrow of his life.

(9:3) Passion and sorrow seek maximum expression. Like a new Moses—who begged God: "If you would only forgive their sin! If you will not, then strike me out of the book that you have written" (Ex 32:32)—Paul would like to sacrifice himself for his people. He would wish to be separated from Christ if he were thereby able to unite his people with Christ! What does that mean for Paul, who speaks so often of "being in Christ," in whom Christians must live? Of course Paul knows that one cannot barter with grace and election but he uses this extreme expression and metaphor in order to declare his bond with Israel. He acknowledges Israel as his brethren. It is true that Paul often speaks of the new worldwide brotherhood in the Spirit which unites Christians (see under 1:13). But he already belongs beforehand and forever by natural descent to that other brotherhood which is Israel. He will not let himself be separated from his people, and he has good reason to say so. The Jews hate him as an alleged traitor to his people and his brethren for he proclaims that Jesus is the Messiah, that Israel's prerogative as the exclusive people of salvation has elapsed, and that Gentiles have the same claims to salvation as Jews. They further reproach him for abolishing the law of Moses for he denies the necessity and value of the Old Testament law. Thus he is abused and persecuted as an apostate and renegade. But he asserts also to the Gentiles his faithfulness to his people. They can be tempted to look arrogantly down upon the rejected Jews (11:13–32). For that reason he acknowledges Israel also before Gentiles and Gentile Christians. Thus Paul says to all who pass judgment upon him: he does not belong to those who trample under foot what was once sacred to them—they are distasteful, to be sure. Rather he has always pursued one and the same goal: to hear God's call and to obey it.

(9:4) The fact that he is a Jew is always a high honor for Paul for by this means he belongs to a people of ancient nobility. They are Israelites, i.e. they have the name which God gave to Jacob and on which the blessing remains.[1] Paul unfolds the full abundance of the riches contained in the name Israel and displays it once again before the possession passes over to the Gentiles. Israel is the sonship, for God calls Israel his own son (Ex 4:22: "Thus says the Lord: Israel is my son, my first-born"). Israel is God's chosen people and property in an incomparable way. Israel's is the glory. Paul recalls the Old Testament reports on how God's majesty lived in the column of fire in Israel's midst and protected his people. God went along on the march through the wilderness (Ex 40:34–38). He reigned over the Ark of the Covenant in the sign of the merciful presence of God (Lev 9:6,23). He filled up the Temple in Jerusalem (Is 6:1:4). The covenants belong to Israel for God concluded and renewed again and again the covenant with his people, with Noah, Abraham and Moses. To Israel belongs the law for God gave it to Israel through Moses. With it Israel had its ancient sacred order (see under 7:1). And God had taught and prepared for Israel the true divine worship which shone forth wonderfully pure and noble vis-à-vis the abomination which Israel observed on all sides in the cults of the heathen peoples. Israel is marked out by the promises of the Messiah and of the messianic age of salvation which God promised to the people so often, again and again, since the time of the forefathers.

(9:5) At the beginning of the history of Israel stand the great holy forefathers, the heroes, with whom God himself spoke and in whose history he wondrously held sway. The forefathers are not merely history, however, but present possession. Israel may always trust in the merits and representative accomplishments of her ancestors. "For the sake of the forefathers' merits take pity on thy people" cry the prayers of Israel. But finally and above all: out of Israel comes the Messiah. Israel has awaited him and Paul can only bear witness that Israel's hope was true, for it has been fulfilled. But he must so speak about the manner of the fulfillment that he cuts himself off from Israel. It is certain that Jesus is the Son of Israel according to human, historical descent. But the same Christ comes also from God as his Son; truly he is the presence of the all-powerful, blessed God himself. As the manifestation of God and in his divinity[2] he is necessarily above everything and everybody, above all history and all peoples, above Jews and Gentiles. For that reason he must be the Christ not only of Israel but also of the Gentiles. He is Savior and Lord in all ages.

Paul closes the enumeration of Israel's honors and the

view over Israel's history with a glorification of the God who reigns over all. He thus speaks of Israel not with hopeless despair but by praising and thanking God. God's grace holds sway always and everywhere. Thus Paul trusts and knows that Israel will finally find salvation also (11:25f).

(9:6) Israel's history gives rise to an agonizing question: what does God's word mean? If Israel does not attain faith and misses salvation then what of God's promises which were given to this people? The Gentiles on the other hand, who have received no promises, who have no patriarchs as bearers of the blessing, are to share in multitudes in the salvation which has appeared in Christ. Is God's word still valid and operative? Or does it not seem to be impotent and unfaithful? The question is puzzling and difficult for Paul. It is difficult for him both as a Jew who loves his people and as a Christian apostle who is to proclaim the word of God.

The question has not become easier today, two thousand years later. It may still be asked of all the honors of Israel mentioned in 9:4. What becomes of the name of Israel? From the first-born son have come the Jews whom one ridicules or even exterminates. Are the covenants still valid? Or is the homeless, buffeted people abandoned by God? The sacred Law became the Talmud, distrusted as primitive or immoral. The sacrificial cult has long since ceased. Israel may now only stand on the wailing wall, as the ruins of her sanctuary, and today not even that. What good are the forefathers? Are they not in the end mythical figures whose very existence is not even certain, and whose ethics and faith in God appear quite questionable?

Paul finds the answer to the questions in Israel's concept of God. God's word endures forever and God's word is spiritual, like himself. For that reason it can never mean anything fleshly or be identical with it and reach its goal within it. And God is always the sovereign Lord who elects freely and who freely leads his word and his work to completion. God's election is never a certain possession of salvation at one's disposal, on which one could rest. To belong to the national and thus merely fleshly community of Israel is still nothing decisive. Natural sonship does not yet make the true Jew. Paul shows from Israel's history that God has always acted in this way and proves it in 9:7–33 with many examples and quotes from the Old Testament. He is here practicing a careful scriptural interpretation as he had learned to do in the rabbinical school.

(9:7) One example is the story of Abraham. Abraham had his first-born son, Ismael, by natural descent, from his maid Agar (Gen 21). When Sara had also borne Abraham a son, Isaac, she demanded from Abraham that he should send away his son born of Agar along with his mother. Abraham resisted but God appeared to him and said: "Heed all that Sara says to you; for through Isaac shall your posterity bear your name" (i.e. only he is of your family who is called Isaac). Ismael, although he stems from Abraham, does not receive the name of honor of Abraham's stock.

(9:8) Thence it follows: corporal descent did not make one a true son of Abraham and corporal sonship in Israel does not yet make one a chosen son of God (9:4). Rather only those chosen by God according to the word and the grace of the promise are the true Israel.

(9:9) Isaac was such a son of the promise. According to Gen 18 God promised this child to Abraham and Sara in their old age, when they had already acquiesced in the unfruitfulness of their marriage, and thus by his will called him into life. It was not nature but God's promise that was here at work. This true sonship of Abraham was not established by the will of the father but by the promise and election of God. God's free will and call were decisive then as henceforth. God's children always arise from the creative summoning word of God. Ismael, stemming only corporally from Abraham, was not the true summoned son. Now all of Israel is certainly descended from Abraham but it is at first only corporal descent. Such descendants are not yet the true Israel intended by God. For this reason the disbelief and the condemnation of Israel are no proof of the failure of God's word. It did not mean the corporal posterity of Abraham at all. God calls his true people and separates it out for himself, cutting across all natural relations of descent.[3]

(9:10) A second example from the Old Testament, the story of Esau and Jacob, the twin sons of Isaac and Rebecca, makes it still clearer that with God not natural descent but the freedom of his elective and creative word is decisive. In the case of Ismael and Isaac one could still object: Isaac alone stems from Sara, the legitimate princely spouse, and Ismael from Agar, the maidservant, the concubine. It was on this account that the divine choice took in the one and not the other. This election thus takes account of human value and human significance. In the case of Esau and Jacob this objection is impossible. Both are descended from one and the same mother; as twins they even originate from one and the same moment of conception.

(9:11f) Furthermore one cannot object here that the one was taken in for having done good and the other rejected for having done evil. For already before their birth, before they themselves had opportunity for any decision or deed, God determined that the first-born was to be the slave of the younger, contrary to the natural priority of primogeniture. Thus it does not depend on the works of man. The will of God, according to his free election, is alone decisive. This will of God, however, remains always the same and always operates in history in the same way. It revealed itself for the first time in the story of Isaac, then anew in the story of Jacob. It will endure and continue to operate through the whole history of salvation, just as it has its effect even now in the present.

(9:13) The fact that and the manner in which God in his love is the free and sovereign Lord is inconceivable for man, but it is the divine reality. This love has its mysteries and abysses just as every love has. Paul establishes this with a saying from the prophet Malachias (1:2f): "Jacob I have loved, but Esau I have hated." What the prophet says, and the apostle quotes in agreement, is no insignificant statement for it speaks not only of God's love but also of hate as its opposite. For a correct understanding of the statement the following should be taken into account: in such polar formulations hating is often only the negation of loving and then means not loving (Lk 14:26; 1 Jn 4:20). In the threat in Mal 1:2f Esau is the Edomite people seized by the judgment of God—not without guilt but because of its malice. The punishment of Esau=Edom is in the prophet's decreeing not eternal condemnation but temporal punishment (Mal 1:4). In any case Paul may not be understood to have taught that God predetermined man for salvation or disaster. He wants only to testify to the freedom of God, by virtue of which God can here and now elect a man, here and now pass over a man. With this statement the demanding claim of the Jews, as if God had to separate out the Jewish people as a race, should be dismissed. The apostle wants to safeguard God's grace as grace, as free giving and acting, against every pretentious human misunderstanding. Paul nowhere states that the eternal decision about a man would ever be made without this man having made his own decisions and performed his own deeds. But he certainly states the contrary when he always exhorts to moral action and reminds of the judgment, which will be a judgment of good and evil deeds (2:6). And if Israel now stands in the role of the "hated Esau" then Paul says first of all that Israel has become guilty in its unbelief (10:14-21), and he then proclaims the mystery that at the end of time all of Israel will find salvation (11:26f).

(9:14) If God treats man as Mal 1:2f says he does then is there not, the brooding intellect asks, injustice and arbitrariness in his ways? God's freedom is, it is true, a question and a stumbling block for human thinking and its concept of justice. Paul gives the question the right to express itself.

(9:15) Yet how does the apostle reply? Does he prove

God's justice? No! He merely shows with further examples from sacred history that God acts in this way. Why God acts in this way man is not capable of knowing. The reasons for his action are God's mystery. Man must be satisfied to know and to believe that justice exists with God. He cannot know what possibilities God has beyond those conceivable to man. He cannot "measure with a tailor's yardstick" the justice and righteousness of God.

With two further sayings of God Paul reveals the elective love and the condemning omission of God (9:13). For the former he points to the powerful saying of Moses: God's compassion is free. Moses had begged God to move with him, thus remaining in the midst of the people. But even vis-à-vis the request of his servant, Moses, God reserves his freedom (Ex 33:19). How much more must that hold true for everyone else.

(9:16) Where it is a question of God's compassion no human work means anything. Using the image of running on a track, Paul says: with however great effort man may strive toward the goal of being favored, reaching this goal does not depend on human effort and desire but on God's will. Paul is certain beyond all doubt that even if man cannot understand it God is still the eternally merciful God. This remains forever man's confidence and consolation. But God is the God of Mercy in freedom; man can force no obligations onto him. The sense of God's freedom, however, is not arbitrary, indiscriminate selection but salvation through grace.

(9:17) The other example is: God's freedom to show mercy also proves itself in the freedom to refuse mercy and to harden man. This is to be discerned from what the Scripture reports about the Pharao (Ex 9). He boasts of his power and strength and believes himself able to wage war with God. He despises the command, conveyed to him repeatedly as the word of God, to let the people Israel go out of Egypt. He thinks he can defy God and does not know that he is nevertheless only fulfilling God's plans, that he is guided by God's will and God is dealing with him. God has let him appear in his time and history and he holds him fast in his obduracy. He must serve as God's instrument so that God's power will be revealed. God's judgment on Pharao will take place in his destruction. With the news of it God's name will be proclaimed in the whole world as that of the almighty Lord.

(9:18) According to the total teaching of Paul, which must also hold true here, it is established as a fact for him that there is no condemnation by God without human responsibility and guilt (2:6–10). But divine condemnation includes human opposition, just as God in general encompasses all human life and existence. This is biblical belief about God (Ps 138:5: "Behind me and before, you hem me in and rest your hand upon me"). To this extent it is God who both takes pity on men and hardens them. But once again the Old Testament story in Paul's exposition is supposed to illuminate what is now happening to Jews and Gentiles. God has taken pity upon the Gentiles and hardened the Jews. But Israel's present stubbornness is not yet final condemnation for the ultimate goal of God's action is Israel's salvation (11:25f).

(9:19) There arise questions which are not easy to

answer. How can God pronounce man guilty, judge and punish him, if God's overwhelming will determines man? How then can man still be made responsible?

(9:20) Paul does not answer this question with theoretical discussions and proofs but tries with other questions to bring questioning man to his senses and to the insight that God is the vastly Mysterious One with whom man cannot argue, but before whom he can only be silent in prayer and trust. Does man perhaps want to try to approach God on the same level in order to debate with him, demanding an answer, as two men of equal rights do? Yet man stands as a creature before the Creator-God as a figure before the sculptor. It would be unheard of if a figure should thus want to reproach the sculptor: why have you made me in this manner?

(9:21) Man before the Creator is like clay in the hand of the potter. The potter can make whatever he wants from the lump of clay, both costly vases for honorable use and vessels for humble service. Thus does God have freedom in his dealing with man: he can elect and condemn. Paul uses here a comparison[4] known to his readers from the Old Testament (Is 64:7; Jer 18:6). To that extent he gives to those who with him acknowledge the Old Testament as the word of God the answer to difficult questions with a scriptural proof. The apostle wants to establish and strengthen the fundamental sentiment of all piety that man must submit to the fact that he is a creature, that he stands not above but under the will of God whose reasons and intentions are a mystery to him. Yet what Paul says elsewhere also remains valid though he does not speak of it here: that in condemnation a judgment on the deeds of man also always takes place, and that in the end God is still the great God of mercy whose will to salvation includes everyone.[5]

(9:22) Paul now applies the previously uttered general statements to the concrete question in front of him and the Church, the question of synagogue and Church. Just as the potter builds costly and ordinary vessels from the clay, so does God. The precious vessels created by him make up the Church and are summoned from among Jews and Gentiles. The other vessels are destined for God's wrath and for destruction. They are Jews and Gentiles outside the community of faith.[6] But God's dealing is different than man's would be and different from what man would expect it to be. Although these vessels were completed ready-made for judgment and downfall God has not surrendered them to destruction. Rather he has put up with them in great patience and long-suffering, i.e. he has let them live, and he will put up with them further. Applied to Israel, of whom Paul is speaking, this means: Israel in her unbelief and hardening does not suffer what she would have earned. God puts up with this Israel until the end of time, when she too will enter into salvation (11:25f).

(9:23f) And God puts up with the unbelieving world so that in the interval of patient waiting he may practice the wealth of his glorious grace on the vessels of his compassion. During the period when the judgment is still withheld God bestows his merciful love, such as the Church called from the Jews and Gentiles is now experiencing it. It is therein that the overflowing abundance of God reveals itself: that his election does not remain within the bounds of the people of Israel but includes all peoples.

(9:25f) Verses 9:25–29 bring forth out of the Sacred Scripture the concluding proof for what has been said. The original question of the epistle (9:6) was whether the old promises and the word of God to Israel still hold good. But now Paul proves precisely from the word of God in Scripture that God had determined the process of salvation history from time immemorial. The prophets already announce the calling of the Gentiles (9:25f) and of only a minority out of Israel (9:27–29).

Paul finds (9:25) the calling of the Gentiles expressed in the prophet Osee 2:1 and 2:25. The prophet speaks of how God seeks and fetches home the lost people of Israel. Then as now the same loving action of God is at work. God now leads the Gentiles home into his kingdom; peoples, who until now appeared forgotten and lost, experience God's love and become his peoples. He is always the God who possesses life and gives it freely.

(9:26–28) The other part of the happening, that only a small portion of the Jews will believe, is also willed by God. Paul also finds this foretold by the prophets. Isaias (10:22f) speaks of it and other prophets after him say again and again that not all of Israel but only a small remnant of the people will be saved. But this is happening now, for God is fulfilling to Israel his word that he has promised salvation. But he "cuts it short," he abridges it; that is, out of the great mass of Israel only a small part is saved.

(9:29) If God did not leave behind at least a part Israel would have to suffer complete destruction, as did Sodom and Gomorrah. Thus God has promised nothing more than that in the messianic age of salvation a small part of Israel will be saved, as is now taking place. God's word is thus true and trustworthy.

(9:30) If one sums up, what one finds is against all probability. There are the Gentiles who in the somber illumination of 1:18–32 stand under the judgment of impiety and sin. They have not really striven after holiness. And there are the Jews, the people of the law, who since antiquity have pursued holiness through the law to the point of exhaustion. The result is strange, even shocking. The runners go away empty-handed while those who did not run reach the goal of holiness. For this holiness is not reached through one's own works but is freely given to faith. For this reason the Gentiles obtain sanctification without works (3:21–31).

(9:31) Israel has the law, the goal of which is sanctification, and she ran after this goal with all her strength. What trouble she takes upon herself for countless generations in order to fulfill the demands of the law! Israel's martyrs have acknowledged the law of the forefathers but Israel has not reached the goal of the law.

(9:32) How is this possible? Israel has thought and striven to become just before God by means of the deeds of the law, thus of her own accomplishment. Israel has refused to follow the way of faith which God has established. She wanted her own works instead of God's gift. The Jews stumbled on God's will to salvation as on a stone.

(9:33) Once more Paul demonstrates with God's word from the Old Testament that it was thus God's plan for salvation. Already in Isaias (8:14; 28:16) God says that he will erect a precious, selected stone on the sacred mountain, Sion. It will be both a cornerstone, on which one builds and a stumbling block on which one is ruined. Paul discloses how this prophecy has been fulfilled in Christ. God is the rock of salvation history; upon him the Church is built. Whoever holds to Christ in faith will not be ruined in the judgment. But for Israel the same Christ has become the stumbling block. Israel rejects her Messiah and in her unbelief she is thereby ruined.[7]

2 ISRAEL'S RESPONSIBILITY

10:1–21

10: 1 Brothers, my heart's desire and my prayer are directed to God in their behalf for their salvation.

2 I bear them witness that they have zeal for God, though a zeal that is unenlightened.

3 Ignorant of the sanctification provided by God and seeking to establish their own, they have not submitted to the sanctification provided by God.

4 Christ has put an end to the Law and has opened the way to sanctification for everyone who believes.

5 Moses writes that the man who realizes that holy living which is required by the Law shall find life by it (Lev 18:5).

6 But the sanctification that comes of faith says, "Do not say in your heart: Who shall ascend into heaven?" (Dt 30:12) (that is, to bring Christ down);

7 or, "Who shall descend into the abyss?" (Ps 106:26) (that is, to bring Christ up from the dead).

8 But what does the Scripture say? "The message is near
you, on your lips and in your heart" (Dt 30:14) (that
is, the message of faith, which we preach).

9 For if you confess with your lips that Jesus is the Lord,
and believe in your heart that God raised him from the
dead, you shall be saved.

10 Because with the heart a man believes and attains holiness, and with the lips profession of faith is made and
salvation secured.

11 "No one who believes in him," says the Scripture, "shall
be disappointed" (Is 28:16).

12 There is no distinction between Jew and Greek. There is
the same Lord of all, generous toward all who call upon
him,

13 since "whoever calls on the name of the Lord shall be
saved" (Joel 3:5).

14 How, then, are people to call upon him in whom they
have not attained faith? And how can they attain faith
in him whom they have not heard? And how are they to
hear if no one preaches?

15 And how are men to preach unless they be sent? As it is
written,
"How welcome is the coming of those who
proclaim the Good News" (Is 52:7).

16 But not all have submitted to the Good News. So Isaias
says,
"Lord, who has believed our preaching?"
(Is 53:1).

17 Faith, then, depends on hearing, and hearing on Christ's
teaching.

18 But I ask: Have they heard? Yes, assuredly,
"Their voice is gone forth into all the earth
and their words unto the ends of the world"
(Ps 18:5).

19 But I say: Has not Israel understood? First of all, Moses
says,

"I will provoke you to jealousy of those who
are not a people:
I will stir you to anger against a senseless nation" (Dt 32:21).
20 Then Isaias dares to say,
"I was found by those who did not seek me;
I revealed myself to those who made no
inquiry about me" (Is 65:1).
21 But to Israel he says,
"All the day I stretched out my hands
to a people unbelieving and contradicting"
(Is 65:2).

In Rom 9 God's will and his election or condemnation were revealed as the ultimate causes of the separation between belief and unbelief. But it had to be said
again and again that God never condemns where there is
no offense. What is seen from God's eternity as the salvation or condemnation of man appears also in time and
history as the obedience and disobedience of man. Thus
Paul also shows Israel's offense. It is the offense of the Jews
that they do not believe God's gospel, do not accept God's
justification, and want to bring about their justification
themselves through works. It is thus an unusual offense, for
Israel did not fail in her moral duty. But here an excess
became the offense. With her own effort out of her own
strength Israel wanted to find a way around God, who
alone can give salvation. Israel has thereby forgotten and
denied the mystery of his election, which is grace. She tries
to change the meaning of his blessing into her own merit
and grandeur and to work his salvation out of her own
capacity. In 10:1-13 Paul shows that the Holy Scripture
of the old covenant already proclaimed justification through

faith as the way of salvation; and in 10:14–21 that Israel's unbelief was already prophesied in the Old Testament.

(10:1) With a direct and profound outbreak of emotion Paul acknowledges Israel as the people of his forefathers and brothers. He will not let himself be separated from this people either before men or before God. His wishes, his love, his prayers belong to Israel and he struggles for her salvation. It becomes clear how he understands it when he says in 9:13: God hated Israel like Esau; and in 9:18: God hardened Israel like the Pharao's heart. If Paul prays for Israel then her fate is not decided by God with final condemnation. This hate and this hardening do not mean that God predetermined Israel to eternal punishment. That is always decided in part by man's decision.

"Paul has led the Church in the prayer for Israel. If the Church should abandon it, it would abandon itself."

(10:2) Paul testifies to his esteem for Israel's piety and zeal for the law. Here is an earnestness of religion, submission in the service of God and zeal for God's honor. Paul would thus not concede that Jewish piety is empty superficiality or even hypocrisy, as we are so quickly tempted to claim.

(10:3) But Paul must add that it was and is zeal without real understanding. The Jews did not want to accept God's justification, which was to be given to them, but wanted to establish their own justification. To let oneself be given God's justification through faith would mean to admit one's own poverty, one's own incapacity and one's dependence on God, and to acknowledge God's abundance and superior strength. It would mean acknowledging oneself a sinner and placing oneself among sinners. Israel's lack of understanding is thus not an excusable error but guilt because it is pride and willfulness before God and opposition and rebellion against him. In zeal for God—Paul states it here once and for all—there can also be profound self-deception and selfishness. There can be zeal for God which does not seek God's honor but rather its own.

Does Paul not give here a diagnosis of Jewry which moves us to further meditation? Israel is truly zealous about God. It is not insignificant when one can say that about a people. That is the glory of Jewry. But is it not true that the Jew is thereby zealous about his own honor? Does Paul do the Jewish people wrong when he claims that Jewish piety also wants to affirm the justification earned through works before the world and before God? Does what he say not also hold true for the unbelieving Jew in a remarkable way? Is it not the unbelieving Jew who so often wants to procure justification in the world from his own strength, after he has abandoned belief in the justification originating from God? We may think of the international effort of the Jewish people for political and social justification in the world. Not a few of the great leading socialists and pacifists have been Jews. Often enough, with profound zeal and earnestness, they take great pains over justice and peace in the world. But is not the zeal often enough without insight; in other words, utopian?

(10:4) It is disobedience and pride if Israel, now that Christ's work of salvation is completed, still wants to follow the Old Testament law in order to hold fast to her justification by works. The law was to lead Israel toward Christ. The law was the "attendant on the way to Christ" (Gal 3:24). In Christ the Old Testament law has arrived at its goal and conclusion. He brings to those who accept him the justification which the Old Testament has promised and striven for. Israel has forgotten that. She has always taken pains with the law in order to attain justification. But she has not understood that the real meaning of the law lies outside and beyond the law itself, in Christ.[8]

(10:5) Once more Paul wishes to show that the word of God of the old covenant already points away from the law toward the way of salvation through faith. Moses says (Lev 18:5) that the man who fulfills all of God's commandments and laws will attain life. Yet who is capable of really fulfilling the law (cf. 3:10)? Attaining justification through the observance of the law is thus only a theoretical possibility.

(10:6) In this light what the same Moses says about justification by faith as another possibility is brought all the more clearly into relief. When he laid the law before the people Moses said (Dt 30:12–14): this law is easy to follow and to attain and does not surpass one's strength. Paul interprets the saying of Moses with reference to its validity in the present.[9] Then it means: in order to possess and to fulfill the law you need not ascend into heaven and descend into the underworld (Ps 106:26) for Christ has come down from heaven and, in his resurrection, has come back from the dead for you. And the word of God which summons to faith in Christ is always near you in the preaching of the Church. Thus you do not need to seek it laboriously like the Jew who takes pains about the learned interpretation of his law.

Faith is at once the easiest and the most difficult thing.

The easiest because God has already done the essential part. The most difficult because man—as precisely the unbelief of Israel shows—in order to attain God in faith must abandon all idols, even the most dear, his own will and his own boasting.

(10:9f) Whoever accepts this word (10:8), confesses it with his lips and believes it with his heart will be saved. The confession reads: Jesus is the Lord (cf. Phil 2:11), for this confession expresses the divine majesty and glory of Christ. Lord, by itself, was the title of God in the Greek Bible of the Old Testament which Jews and Christians used. Yet at that time the gods of the Gentiles, both in heaven and on earth (i.e. the emperors), were called and acknowledged in this way. The acknowledgment of Christ as the Lord thus has its special emphasis and direction for both the Jews and the Gentiles.[10] But the decisive statement of faith is that Christ has died and is risen. Therein are enclosed the redemption and the new life and, in this case, the elevation of Christ to the reigning power over the universe. Whoever places himself under this power in faith will attain salvation.

(10:11) Already through the prophet Isaias God has revealed the decisive significance of faith. The prophet says (Is 28:16) that the believer will not stand ashamed in the last judgment but will experience salvation.

(10:12f) This way of salvation and this offer of salvation hold good for all men. "All" means here the Jews and Greeks since the world breaks down into these two parts in regard to the history of salvation (cf. 1:14 and 1:17). Thus for the Jew also the demand for laborious justification through the law is no longer valid; rather the offer of justification by faith. One and the same way of salvation must be open to all men simply because the same Lord and God rules over them all. This one God is rich enough to bestow his gifts upon them all. The profound and comforting declaration of God's abundance is very dear to Paul. Let us not forget it! Paul praises the abundance of God in Rom 2:4; 9:23; 11:33; Eph 2:4; Phil 4:19. Christ the Lord is also rich (Eph 3:8) and from the poverty into which he entered (2 Cor 8:9) the Church was enriched (1 Cor 1:5).

(10:14f) Paul is still (see under 8:9 and 9:6) pursuing the question: is God's word true and valid if Israel does not attain the promised salvation? Therefore Paul now shows (10:14–21) that the word of God in the Old Testament already knew and proclaimed in advance the present-day history of Israel. For it says that Israel will be able to hear the gospel but that she will not obey the message, and therefore the preaching of the gospel will pass from Israel to other peoples. In these verses Paul assembles selected Old Testament quotes in deliberate and artistic order, taking up again the preaching of the prophets. They already had to accuse Israel of constant opposition against God. They already went from unbelieving Israel to the Gentiles.

Israel was also able to attain faith. All the prerequisites which are demanded for it have come to pass for Israel. Paul enumerates these prerequisites successively, in a chain. The series begins with the most recent link and leads back to the earliest one: God can only be called upon where people believe in him. The gospel can only be believed where it is heard. It can only be heard when it is preached.

It can only be preached by those who were sent out to do so. All these conditions for being able to believe were fulfilled for Israel. To Israel came the messengers sent out and empowered by God. The beautiful saying of the prophet Isaias (52:7) about the messengers who run in joyful haste to deliver their message was fulfilled. These messengers of joy are there now in Israel. Truly, the apostles and teachers of the Church go out in all directions to bring the Good News of salvation.

(10:16) Israel was able to hear and believe, yet she was not willing. It is still the same unbelief of Israel that the prophet Isaias experienced toward his preaching; the unbelief of which he had to accuse Israel and which forces out of him the reproachful question before God (Is 53:1): "Lord, who has believed our preaching?"

(10:17) Israel had the opportunity to understand the message of the gospel for the Jews were and are able to hear the preaching of the apostles. And in the preaching of the apostles—thus Paul says in serious terms—Christ himself is speaking, he himself summons to faith through the preaching of the Church. Likewise Paul repeatedly says that the preaching of the apostles is the word of God himself; thus 2 Cor 5:20; 13:3; 1 Thess 2:13. Thus the word of God and the word of Christ himself is heard. For this reason it is well founded and correct when we also call a present-day sermon—no matter how mediocre it may be—simply the word of God, just as we also characterize hearing a sermon as hearing the word of God.

Israel cannot maintain that she was unable to hear the gospel. Paul describes the progress of the gospel throughout

the entire world with a verse from Psalms (18:5). It has
penetrated to the furthest extremity of the world. Thus
Israel was also able to hear. What a powerful conviction
declares itself in this statement by the apostle! Naturally
Paul sees the world within the boundaries of the Roman
world-empire of that time, not as the globe with six conti-
nents. But he says that the entire Roman Empire has heard
the message. Yet what is the situation of the Church and
of her mission at the time of the apostle? There are Christian communities in several large cities, yet they are but
small bands and few people are aware of their existence. The
broad hinterland has still hardly been touched by the mission. Great countries with rich cultures in Egypt and Spain
still lie outside the mission. But Paul is convinced that the
fire if it is kindled in only a few places will quickly spread
(as in fact actually happened, according to evidence from
early Christian missionary history). Thus the apostle can
express the forceful certainty of the Church: the struggle
for the peoples of the earth is already decided! The gospel
came to them all!

(10:19) Nor can Israel maintain that she was unable to
understand the message of the gospel. Israel was able to
and had to understand if she only wanted to. Paul shows
this with two scriptural passages. A statement of Moses has
come true which says (Dt 32,21): God will embitter Israel
and make her jealous of those who are not a people (i.e.
the Gentiles who, according to Old Testament linguistic
usage, are not called a people since only the one chosen
people may bear the honorary name of people) and who are
a senseless nation. This is now taking place since the Gen-

tiles are summoned and attain the blessings of salvation while Israel is embittered and jealous that the Gentiles are to be preferred to her. Thus even the senseless nonpeople of the Gentiles understands the message. How much more would Israel understand it if she were only willing!

(10:20) Isaias 65:1 testifies to the same thing for he says that God let himself be found even by those who did not seek him and was revealed to those who made no inquiry about him. This is now taking place, for the Gentiles who did not worry about God are entering the community of salvation of the Church. And again the apostle's conclusion is the same: if even the Gentiles heard God's voice in the gospel and found him how much more should Israel have understood the gospel and found God—Israel, for ages enlightened by her prophets, elected and sustained by God's love, if only Israel had been willing to understand!

(10:21) But the same Isaias (65:2) also tells whereby Israel was ruined: by the disobedience and contradiction with which she responded to God's constant loving solicitation.

Chapter 10 of the Epistle to the Romans is an essential complement to chapter 9. In chapter 9 Paul first answered man's grumbling question about God's ways with the proclamation of God's sovereignty to which man must submit. In chapter 10 Paul now adds: Israel's history and fate have not only been a judgment on Israel but also a decision in Israel and by Israel herself. It is not only a question of God's electing and ruling will but also of Israel's choice and decision for unbelief. All history between salvation and perdition is both God's will and action and man's life, for which he must account. These may be antitheses which in calculation come together with difficulty or not at all but the believer knows that in faith and in the life based on faith they are real.

3   ISRAEL'S REMNANT TODAY

11: 1–24

11: 1 I ask then: Has God cast off his people? By no means! Why, I myself am an Israelite, of the posterity of Abraham, of the tribe of Benjamin.

2 God has not cast off his people whom he foreknew. Or do you not know what the Scripture says in the account of Elias, how he lodges complaint with God against Israel?

3   "Lord, they have slain your prophets,
       They have razed your altars,
       and I alone am left,
       And they seek my life" (3 Kings 19:10).

4 But what does the divine answer say to him?
       "I have left myself seven thousand men,
       who have not bent their knees to Baal"
       (3 Kings 19:18).

5 Even so at the present time there is a remnant left, selected by grace.

6 And if by grace, then not in virtue of deeds; otherwise grace would no longer be grace.

7 What then? What Israel is seeking after, that it has not obtained; but the chosen ones have obtained it, and the rest have been blinded,

8 as it is written,
       "God has given them a spirit of stupor
       until the present day,
       Eyes that they may not see,

and ears that they may not hear" (Dt 29:3; Is 29:10).

9 And David says,

"Let their table become a snare and a trap and a stumbling block and a retribution unto them.

10   Let their eyes be darkened that they may not see, and let them bow their backs forever" (Ps 68:23f).

11 I ask then: Have they so stumbled as to fall utterly? By no means! But by their false step salvation has come to the Gentiles, that they may emulate them.

12 Now if their false step is directed to the enrichment of the world, and their defection to the enrichment of the Gentiles, how much more their full number!

13 Now I say to you Gentiles: As long surely as I am an Apostle of the Gentiles, I shall do honor to my ministry,

14 in the hope that I may provoke to emulation those who are my own flesh and may save some of them.

15 If the rejection of them leads to the reconciliation of the world, what will taking them back lead to but life from the dead?

16 Now if the first cake of the dough is holy, so too is the batch of dough; and if the root is holy, so too are the branches.

17 But if some of the branches have been broken off, and if you, a wild olive, are grafted in their place, and have become a partaker of the root and richness of the olive tree, do not boast against the branches.

18 But if you do boast notwithstanding, remember that it is not you who support the root, but the root you.

19 You will say, then, "Branches were broken off, that I might be grafted in."

20 True, but they were broken off because of unbelief, whereas you because of faith hold your position. Be fearful, not conceited,

21 because if God has not spared the natural branches, perhaps he may not spare you either.

22 See, then, the goodness and the severity of God: his
severity toward those who have fallen, but the goodness
of God toward you if you abide in his goodness; otherwise you will also be cut off.

23 But they too, if they do not continue in unbelief, will
be grafted in; certainly God is able to graft them back.

24 Why, if you have been cut off from the wild olive tree
which is natural to you, and, contrary to nature, have
been grafted into the cultivated olive tree, how much
more shall these, the natural branches, be grafted into
their own olive tree!

The question of the destiny of Israel is clarified for
the past. How and why everything took place in this
way is now evident. The question now turns forward, from
the present to the future. What else will happen to Israel?
Paul is able to give an answer to this question in Rom 11.
He discloses God's plan for salvation and sketches prophetically, in the most general outlines, God's future ways with
mankind. The apostle also sees in the future the salvation
of Israel become full. In the present at least a remnant of
Israel attains faith. Meanwhile the Gentile peoples enter
the Church. Israel will follow after them at the end.

(11:1) Out of the gloomy statements of chapters 9 and 10
the question finally arises of whether God has rejected his
people forever. Has he taken back election and promise?
Some people may have once asked this question, just as
there are yet many Christians and pagans who say this con-
sciously or unconsciously. Is Jewry not oppressed among
peoples everywhere, buffeted, despised and excluded from
the community? But Paul—and with him the New Testament—answers such a question forcibly and categorically.
No! As proof Paul names first his own person and his fate.

Paul is a Jew who boasts of being the son of Abraham and a member of the Jewish national community (cf. Phil 3:5). But faith in Christ has been given to him. Thus it is evident that even today God chooses his believers out of Israel.

(11:2) Thus God does not by any means want to condemn Israel as an entire people. Election and promise remain in force for Israel. Paul is certainly not the only Jew who now experiences grace. It is once more as it was in the time of Elias: that not the entire great multitude of the people but certainly a part is called and elected by God (3 Kings 19:9–18).

(11:3) Elias was once persecuted by his and God's enemies and supposed himself to be the single, last servant of God in a faithless people. In despair he complained to God of his distress.

(11:4) But God's decree (3 Kings 19:18) revealed to him that there were still 7000 servants of God in the nation —a small minority to be sure, but sufficient to pass on and guarantee election and faith in Israel through the ages. Faith and the worship of God, after all, did not die out completely in Israel. Thus God took and takes care of the preservation of his people.

(11:5) A small part of the people was at that time the bearer of the promise. So also is there now a remnant of Israel which is exempted from unbelief. Israel's election is also realized in her today. Today, as once before, not the whole people but only a small minority is the bearer of grace.

(11:6) Thus the same law of the working of salvation always holds true: God calls and elects freely according to his will without any merit of the elect, thus without regard for works accomplished. No man has a claim on God's grace. Thus even Israel cannot claim that because of her many efforts to fulfill the law she should attain salvation before others. Rather God can summon the Gentiles and pass over the greater part of Israel.

(11:7) But then what about the enormous majority of Israel, Israel as a whole, if now only a remnant is saved? Must it be concluded that the largest part is forever rejected and lost? No! They have only been hardened for a time.

(11:8) Even this is dreadful enough. Following the prophets' predictions of disaster (Dt 29:3; Is 29:10), Paul describes this condition of Israel with the severest phrases. The prophets had threatened Israel with disaster for her offense. Now God is letting this punishment come over Israel. He closes the people's eyes so that it no longer sees salvation, and its ears so that it no longer hears the preaching. God does so by letting Israel be caught in her own unbelief. Here again sin is the punishment for sin, just as God abandoned the Gentiles to their sin for punishment (1:24,26,28).

(11:9f) Still gloomier is the saying of David (Ps 68:23f) which must now be fulfilled. The terrible punishment with which the psalm threatened the impious is now being meted out to unbelieving Israel. The table is to become their ruin. The meal which man takes from the table should be a strength and an aid to life for him; the community in which he celebrates the meal should lend him support and protection in time of danger. Yet for Israel everything is to be turned upside down and what should be her strength and aid will result in the opposite. Just as birds become en-

tangled in the snare and become booty so will it go with
Israel. What seems good will becomes for her a treacherous
trap and for her everything will turn into avenging ruin.
Israel will be blind so that she no longer perceives the true
and the good. She will be bowed down, be it under the
slavery which she has to bear, be it under the angry judgment which lies upon her.[11] The Jew Paul, who so loved
his people, was able to apply these severe words to his
people and to find them realized only with the deepest
sorrow.

(11:11) Yet these words are not the last things which
Paul has to say. No word is the end; each in its place is
only the way to be traveled. The goal is the mercy of God
(11:32). Israel's stumbling on the stone of vexation is no
stumbling to final ruin and Israel's fall is not final downfall.
Out of Israel's present unbelief is to come salvation for the
Gentiles and conversion for the Jews. Paul is thinking of
the progress of the mission, for the messengers of faith
respect the Jews' position of precedence and always go first
to the Jews. With most Jews, however, they meet with
opposition and obduracy. This leads to a break with the
synagogue and the missionaries go to the Gentiles. The
Acts of the Apostles often tells of this development. Because of Israel's unbelief the gospel thus reaches the Gentiles. From the unbelief of the former comes the salvation
of the latter. Israel will see this and then recognize that the
God of Israel now becomes the God of the Gentiles, that
Israel's Holy Scriptures bring the Gentiles light and that
Israel's blessing belongs to the Gentiles. Israel should
thereby be led to reflection, be shaken in her mistaken cer-

tainty, come to long for the same blessing and finally be driven herself onto the way of salvation.

(11:12) Because of Israel's refusal and fall grace goes out to the world. Paul concludes: what a blessing for the world it will be when Israel finally comes to the fulfillment of her mission! For this reason the apostle wants to give a warning, especially to Gentiles and Gentile Christians, against despising this people. It is so important for Paul to establish this that, interrupting the continuity, he inserts an exhortation of his own to the Gentile Christians (11:13–24).

(11:13) Paul calls himself with pride an Apostle to the Gentiles, and he is conscious of the grandeur of this duty. According to Gal 2:8f, Paul and the twelve original apostles came to an agreement that they were to devote themselves to the mission among the Jews and he among the Gentiles. But as an apostle to the Gentiles Paul says here something astonishing, even shocking. In all his work and effort among the Gentile peoples he has, ultimately and at bottom, only Israel's rescue in mind. He runs restlessly throughout the world for the sake of the people Israel, which he has left behind and which has thrust him out.

(11:14) For that is always his intention: to make his flesh, the Jews, his brothers according to natural descent, envious of the favored Gentiles (11:11) and thus convert the Jews.

(11:15) The service to the saving of the Jews is nevertheless also service to the salvation of the world. Out of the condemnation of the Jews comes now the reconciliation of the world. When they, having become believers, are welcomed by God it will mean life in exchange for death for the world. Then salvation will dawn for mankind in that it will arise out of its present condition of transitoriness and decay (8:20) to the life of redeemed perfection.

(11:16) Paul illustrates and illucidates Israel's immortal dignity through the two metaphors of the first cake and the batch of dough and of the root and the branches. The apostle first recalls provision of Old Testament law (Num 15:17–21). From the first batch of bread of the new corn harvest the Israelites must bring God a small portion, the first cake, as an offering. The rest of the bread baked from the dough and eventually all bread of the new harvest should thereby be consecrated and holy to God. In her great forefathers who were God's friends—Abraham, Isaac, Jacob, Moses and the others—Israel has a sacred beginning and origin and thereby all of Israel remains forever consecrated and holy to God. The other example is taken from nature: as are the roots so are the trees and branches. The forefathers, as the roots of the people, sanctify forever all its members.

(11:17) Certainly God's grace has now visibly turned from Israel to the Gentiles. This could easily tempt the Gentile Christians to arrogance and to contempt of Israel. They could believe themselves to be the more valuable vis-à-vis Israel. Paul hopes to prevent this with a comparison he develops out of the metaphor of Israel as the sacred root. God has planted a noble olive tree, his people Israel. In the judgment he has cut off several branches. Other branches, formerly wild olives, have been grafted in their place (these are the Christians called from among the Gentile peoples) so that the good saps of the tree now also permeate the former wild olives and ennoble them. Thus the Gentile Christians have received a share in Israel's religious inheritance and possession of salvation. But they have no reason to boast.

(11:18) Israel is and remains the root of the tree, here the Church. The Church rests on Israel's history with God and not on what the Gentiles bring along.

(11:19) The Gentile Christian could object: but God evidently cares more for us than for the Jews. After all, in order to take us in he has excluded the Jews.

(11:20) That may be true, yet no arrogance may come of it. Through unbelief the Jews separated themselves from root and tree and for the sake of their faith the Gentiles were taken in. But faith excludes all arrogance for faith knows that it does not stand by itself but rather by God's grace. For this reason there is always in faith not *Angst* but fear of God.

(11:21) God's action, on which faith knows it is dependent, is free. God has shown this with Israel. He has let his Israel, the chosen people, fall. Must that not warn everyone?

(11:22) God's goodness was revealed in his action toward the Gentile Church, his severity in his action toward Israel. The crucially essential thing is to remain in the goodness and faithfulness of God. Faith does not count on one's own human faithfulness; thus not on one's own virtue but on the faithfulness of God. God's goodness would become God's severity if he who has been favored frivolously disdained the gift of God and abandoned his goodness. Stated metaphorically: the Gentile Christian can be pruned away from the tree once more. For this reason all are exhorted to fear.

(11:23) God is not bound but free. Just as his goodness can become severity so also his severity can become goodness. This applies also to Israel for God's severity can change to goodness if Israel's unbelief mends its ways. Just as the Gentile Christian can once more be pruned out of the trunk so also the Jew can be grafted in again. God is powerful. From a human point of view Israel's situation may be hopeless. Yet from almighty God the great wonder of the future can be awaited—that which has been cut away will grow back in.

(11:24) This wonder of the conversion of Israel would not be as great as the calling of the Gentile Church, for the wild olive (the Gentiles) had been grafted into the noble olive (Israel). This is against all nature. It would be much easier and in accord with nature if the natural branches pruned away were grafted once more into their own parent olive tree. If we read the text closely we notice that Paul no longer says that the pruned branches could be grafted in again but rather that they will be grafted in again. The confidence that Israel will surely experience salvation breaks through.[12]

4 ISRAEL'S FULL NUMBER AT THE END

11:25–36

11:25 I would not, brothers, have you ignorant of this mystery, lest you should have a conceited opinion of yourselves, that a partial blindness only has befallen Israel, until the full number of the Gentiles should enter,

26 and thus all Israel shall be saved, as it is written,

"There will come out of Sion the deliverer,
  he will turn away impiety from Jacob (Is 59:20f);
27 And this is my covenant with them,
  When I shall take away their sins" (Is 27:9).
28 For your sake they are enemies in view of the spread of
 the gospel,
29 but for their fathers' sake they are most dear in virtue
 of the divine choice. For God does not revoke his gifts
 and his call.
30 Just as once you did not believe God, and now have obtained mercy, because of their unbelief;
31 even so they too have not believed on the occasion of the
 mercy shown you, that they too may obtain mercy.
32 For God has imprisoned all mankind in unbelief, that he
 may have mercy on them all.
33 Oh, the depth of the riches and of the wisdom and of the
 knowledge of God! How incomprehensible are his judgments and how unsearchable his ways!
34 For
  "Who has known the mind of the Lord,
  or who has been his counselor? (Is 40:13)
35 Or who has first given to him
  and in turn had a recompense due him?" (Job
  41:3)
36 For from him and through him and unto him are all
 things. To him be glory forever, Amen.

Paul is able to resolve the harassing questioning and
mind racking over Israel's history which fill Rom 9–11
in that he clarifies the mysterious decrees of God from
what divine revelation has disclosed to him. How and when
this happened Paul does not say. But God's revelation must
have ensued in answer to incessant prayer in struggle with
God. Thus the certainty was granted to the apostle that
in the end all Israel will enter into salvation. The question
may arise as to how this is to take place in the fulfillment

of world history. But we may not leave the manner of prophetic prediction out of consideration. The prophet must say and can only say what God commands him. The other is hidden even to him. Thus he can perhaps only announce the "that" but not describe in detail the "how."

(11:25) It is a question of such a detail, as regards the general prophecy, if we want to ask the meaning of the full number of the Gentiles (11:25) and all Israel (11:26). Paul hardly intends to say that all Gentiles and all Jews, in general and without exception, will confess the faith. This must be impossible for the simple reason that Paul reckons with the possibility of an imminent end of time (13:12). Rather the full number determined by God for the end of time will be realized. The measure of time will also then be full.

(11:26f) In the light of God's revelation to him Paul finds the promise of Israel's final salvation already announced in the Old Testament. It is already declared by the prophet (Is 59:20) that Jacob (i.e Israel, whose progenitor was Jacob) will be freed from his impiety (his unbelief) and that God will take away sin from his people and conclude a new covenant with them (Is 27:9). Israel is thus not rejected but only put aside.

(11:28) Paul reflects further on the relative situation of Jews and Gentiles. The Jews certainly stand in opposition to God since they do not believe the gospel; this results in the blessing of the Gentiles because for this reason the gospel passes over to the Gentile peoples. But in ancient times God chose Israel in the person of her great, holy forefathers and God's election and love abide with her forever.

(11:29) God is not like a fickle human being. He is never sorry for his gifts of grace. They are irrevocable. For this reason the greatest grace of Israel, her summoning and election out of the peoples of the earth, must also last.[13] Men's disobedience and sin may be ever so great but God's will to grace will nonetheless attain its goal in the end.[14]

(11:30) All history between God and man is always the same. It always goes from man's disobedience to God's mercy. This holds true for Jews and Gentiles. The Gentiles —they are addressed—were once disobedient since they gave themselves over to idolatry and immorality (1:18–32). Now the Gentiles have found mercy since as a result of the unbelief of the Jews the gospel reached them.

(11:31) The Jews are disobedient while the Gentiles experience mercy. Yet the Jews will also find mercy; Paul dares to say that they already find mercy now. The future with the salvation of Israel is so imminent that Paul considers it already dawned. Paul can speak thus because he expects the end of the present age imminently (13:11), and because of the certainty of the prophets in general. The future as the promised act of God is so certain for him that he can proclaim it as present.

(11:32) The Omnipotent One lets everyone become entangled in disobedience in order to reveal his grace toward them all. All courses and movements of world history finally come to rest when human disobedience is swallowed up in divine mercy.

Whoever reads the exultant closing words of Rom 11

must not forget the words of judgment of Rom 9. But whoever reads Rom 9 with its terrifying statements about God as the Creator in whose hand man is like clay in the hand of the potter; about the vessels of anger next to the vessels of honor which God can form as he will; about the delusion and hardening of man which belongs to God's plan; whoever reads Rom 9 must not arbitrarily stop there and find it stated that from the very beginning God wills the destruction of his creatures. Condemnation is not from the beginning on the reality of this or that particular man, but always only God's possibility, which must of course remain his freedom and his sovereign authority. Rom 9 should humble man in fear under God's freedom and in this fear man should flee to God. Wherever man's every claim on God, with which he would want to bind God, is given up, there may the promise of the goodness and faithfulness of God, with which he binds himself (11:29), be grasped. Whoever has entered into the judgment of God may expect God's mercy.

(11:33) Throughout the three chapters Rom 9–11 Paul struggles with the question of the destiny of Israel. Yet the darkness which lies over it becomes lighter and lighter as he searches and prays. His hope becomes more and more confident until he finally breaks out in the prayerful and joyful glorification of God in 11:33–36.

In God is an unfathomable depth of riches, wisdom and knowledge. He contains possibilities of planning and realization, of knowledge and power, of salvation and love which man cannot surmise. The governing of God leads far beyond all human understanding. The judgments according to which he directs history are for man inscrutable. He has ways of salvation and the power to bring everything to its goal. They are ways which man does not perceive and which he cannot follow.

(11:34) Paul speaks further in scriptural sayings (Is 40:13 and Job 41:3). Who has on his own ever known the thoughts of God? Man only knows them insofar as God reveals them. But then he perceives first of all that they are inscrutable. Or who could ever boast of having sat in God's council?

(11:35) No one can ever render God a service and obligate him thereby to a return of service. For this reason he remains forever, vis-à-vis all creatures, the altogether Free One.

(11:36) God alone is the beginning, direction, and goal of all things and of all history.[15] To him belongs therefore divine glory for all time (cf. 16:27).

In the hymn 11:33–36 the questioning and brain racking of the apostle reaches its conclusion. But he does not stop because all questions were sensibly solved or because provable or proven answers were found. Rather Paul submits to the decree of God in acknowledgement, adoration and praise for he knows and believes that he is the Righteous and the Good.

FOOTNOTES TO CHAPTER IV

1 According to Gen 32:29 God gave Jacob this name: "You shall no longer be called Jacob, but Israel." This name is always the sign of election for Israel; thus in Is 43:1: "Fear not, for I have redeemed you; I have called you by name: you are mine."

2 Paul attributes often, and with unquestionable certainty, divine dignity, nature and rule to Christ. He calls Christ God's own Son (8:32), equal to God (Phil 2:6), the manifestation of God (2 Cor 5:19; Col 1:15; Tit 2:13). It is essentially nothing more when the apostle calls Christ God himself (Rom 9:5), but this is the only place in the epistles of the apostle where he does so explicitly. To this extent Rom 9:5 is of special dogmatic significance.

3 In Gal 4:21–31 Paul has drawn the further conclusions from the story of the sons of Abraham. There he says: Ismael is the prototype of the Jews as a whole since they also, like him, are only naturally descended from Abraham. Isaac, however, is the prototype of the Christians, for they are like Isaac God's children by election and grace. This must have been a truly unbearable claim for the Jews. According to it they are forced by Paul into the position of the illegitimate son of the maidservant, and the Gentiles, despised by the Jews, are supposed to be instead the true sons of Abraham! What struggles and violent emotions Paul must have endured before such an understanding of the history of salvation became visible to him, the proud Jew who passionately loved his people.

4 The impressive image of the potter and the clay as a simile for the relationship of man and Creator is often used in the Old Testament (in Isaias, Jeremias, the Books of Wisdom and in Sirach); then in the literature of the rabbis in Jesus' time and in the re-

cently discovered scrolls of Qumran; but also previously, in old Egyptian and Babylonian texts. The trade of pottery was of incomparably greater significance in antiquity than today, and the potter's doings were known to every man from frequent observation and, therefore, chosen as an example, easily comprehensible.

5 Let it be noted that, as unphilosophical as Paul's phrases sound, even the most modern present-day philosophy and philosophy of religion acknowledge the validity of 9:20f. Here is expressed man's consciousness of being a creature before God, as the mystery before which man subsides in reverence and love (thus, on these verses, Immanuel Kant; Rudolf Otto).

6 Paul's expression is carefully considered. He says of the vessels of mercy that they were predetermined and prepared by God for glory (9:23); of the vessels of wrath only that they are ready for destruction (9:22). Here the assertion of predetermination, thus of the prehistoric determination by God, is lacking. The glorification of the Church is established in advance in the will of God, but in no case did Paul intend to say the same for the perdition of unbelief. He never intended to say that God makes creatures who would be destined from the very beginning according to his will only for his wrath and for destruction. It remains unanswered, by whom the vessels of wrath and destruction are prepared: by God or by men themselves?

7 Paul links two verses of Isaias (8:14 and 28:16) in 9:33. If we look up the Old Testament quotes in the text of the Old Testament we ascertain that here, as in many passages in Paul's epistles, the apostle quotes quite freely. He even permits himself occasionally to change the wording slightly so that the sense of the Old Testament which he intends stands out more clearly. But no one can value the word of God in the Old Testament more highly than Paul, no one feels himself more closely bound to it than he does. He would therefore never permit himself to deal with the word of the Old Testament arbitrarily and unfaithfully. If he allows himself such adaptation of quotes, he does so in the certainty that he is not altering the sense in any way, but rather that it only becomes clearer. It is not the letter which is important for Paul but the spirit.

8 It is true that Paul says at first only of the Old Testament law

that it has found its goal and conclusion in Christ. Theology, however, has added to this phrase an extended discussion about whether it must hold true beyond that, in the sense that in the new covenant all legality is abolished. Paul himself says that even if the many burdensome (Old Testament) regulations are abolished, the sense of the law as divine order nevertheless remains and must be fulfilled (3:31; 8:1, 4; 13:9). Yet in fact it must hold true that the order of the gospel may no longer be constraint of legality but freedom of love.

[9] Again with this interpretation of the Old Testament by Paul it should be mentioned that he deals very freely with the wording of Scripture (see below under 9:33). He links several passages of the Old Testament (Lev 18:5; Dt 30:12–14; Ps 106:26). When Paul examines the Old Testament in the light of the gospel he discovers these verses, which speak of the justification as easy to attain, in contrast to the old justification which demanded an earnest effort. This easily attained justification, however, Paul knows to be given in Christ. When Ps 106:26 speaks of an ascent into heaven and descent into the underworld it reminds the apostle of Christ, who came down from heaven and returned from the underworld of the dead. For this reason he interprets Dt 30:12–14 and Ps 106:26 as referring to Christ and the new covenant's gift of salvation. Besides, Jewry in Paul's time already explained Dt 30:14 as referring to the preaching of the word of God in the synagogue, much as Paul does. When Paul understands Dt 30:14 of the preaching in the Church, he must once more be a pupil of Jewish theology (see under 8:36).

[10] The latter becomes clear, for example, from the martyr deeds of Saint Polycarp, Bishop of Smyrna. The judge demanded that he say: "The emperor is the Lord," and sacrifice. Polycarp unconditionally refused because it would have been an acknowledgment of the god-emperor. Christians are only permitted to acknowledge: Christ is the Lord.

[11] Would we not like to ask whether this threat is fulfilled visibly? Saint Chrystomus already did so in his interpretation of the Epistle to the Romans, for he says (Migne, *Patrologia Graeca* 60:584): "Does the prophecy of the psalm require still another interpretation? When were the Jews as easy to seize as now? When

so easy to ensnare? When has God so bent their backs?" Origen
(Migne, *Patrologia Graeca* 14:1183)warns, however, that we must
not think only of the Jews since the threat could apply to all of us:
"Each one of us must fear that the table of the divine words, from
which we want to take the food of the word of God, becomes for
us a snare or reprisal or downfall, if we do not take for ourselves
therefrom, prudently and purely, as is worthy, pure, spiritual food
of wisdom."

12 Exegesis will rightly notice that the description of grafting and
of the possible cases which Paul mentions are contrary to all practice. One does not graft a wild seedling onto a noble tree (11:17)
and one does not reinsert pruned branches (11:23f). But it is
occasionally so that Paul's metaphors and comparisons are artificial
and forced (see under 7:4).

13 Accordingly Israel is not "the people, which was once the
chosen people," as is sometimes said; rather she is still today the
chosen people.

14 The certainty that Israel will also finally acknowledge Christ
and thus find salvation is also expressed in a saying of Jesus (Mt
23:39). Here Jesus speaks as he leaves the temple and the public in
general: "Yes, I tell you, you will not see me again until you cry
out: 'A blessing on him who comes in the name of the Lord!' "
Thus Israel will also one day greet Jesus as the Blessed One of God
and believe in him.

15 Paul uses a formula of the Greek mysticism and philosophy of
religion of his time. Thus in the second century A.D. the emperor
Marcus Aurelius can say: "O nature! From you, in you, and unto
you are all things!" Here the formula is understood, of course,
pantheistically of nature which, flowing out of God and emptying
into him again, is divine. Paul on the other hand understands the
formula of God, who is revealed in history, yet remains its Lord.
For this reason Paul writes in the second part "through him"
instead of "in him."

V THE CHRISTIAN LIFE

12:1—15:13

It certainly holds true: through the gift of God's grace the justified come into being. And: man is justified by faith without works (3:24). But God's action on man never happens so that man would thereby have no will of his own but only so that man himself acknowledges the act of God with his life and carries it out for himself. God's gift always becomes for man his duty. After Rom 6–8 has sketched the outlines of the human behavior following from the action of God Rom 12–15 will now deal with it thoroughly and with detailed instructions. One would misunderstand Rom 1–11 if one did not necessarily go on to Rom 12–15. One would misunderstand Rom 12–15 if the admonitions of these chapters were to hold good without the presupposition of Rom 1–11.

1 GOD'S GIFT AND MAN'S SERVICE

12:1–21

12: 1 I exhort you, therefore, brothers in view of the mercies of God, to offer your bodies as a sacrifice, living, holy, pleasing to God—such as is the worship of mind and soul.

2 And do not conform to this world's way of life, but be transformed by the renewal of your mind, that you may investigate the will of God—all that is good, all that is acceptable to him, all that is perfect.

3 By the commission that has been given to me, I say to each one among you: Let no one esteem himself more than he ought, but let him esteem himself in moderation according to the degree of faith which God has apportioned to each one.

4 For just as in one body we have many organs, yet not all organs have the same function,

5 so we, the aggregate, are one body in Christ, but individually to one another we stand in the relation of part to part.

6 We have gifts differing according to the grace that has been given us. If the gift is that of God's inspired spokesmen, let it be used in harmony with faith;

7 if it is ministry, let one minister, or if one is a teacher, let him teach;

8 if one's gift is exhortation, let him exhort; let him who gives alms, do so in simplicity; let him who presides, do so with diligence; let him who shows mercy, do so with cheerfulness.

9 Let love be without pretense. Hate what is evil; cling to what is good.

10 Love one another with fraternal charity, anticipating one another with honor.

11 Do not be slothful in zeal; be inflamed in the spirit; serve the age.

12 Rejoice in hope. Be patient in tribulation, persevering in prayer.

13 Relieve the needs of the saints, exercise hospitality with eagerness.

14 Bless those who persecute you; bless and do not curse.

15 Rejoice with those who rejoice; weep with those who weep.

16 Agree in thought with one another, aspiring not to high
   things, but agreeing in thought with lowly people. "Be
   not wise in your own eyes" (Prov 3:7).
17 To no man render evil for evil, but "take thought for
   decent conduct in the sight of all men" (Prov 3:4).
18 If it be possible, as far as lies in your power, be at
   peace with all men.
19 Do not avenge yourselves, beloved, but give place to the
   wrath of God, for it is written,
   "Vengeance is mine; I will repay, says the Lord"
   (Dt 32:35).
20 But
   "If your enemy is hungry, give him food;
      If he is thirsty, give him drink;
   For by so doing you will heap coals of fire on his
      head (Prov 25:21f).
21 Be not conquered by evil, but conquer evil by good.

The great Christian community must preserve and
bring into harmony two different, even contrary rights:
the right of the individual and that of the community. In
the last analysis all the admonitions of Rom 12–15 are
concerned with the correct order of the two.

(12:1) In 12:1f Paul states the basic rule, out of which
the remaining admonitions can develop. At the beginning of
the new, exhortatory main section of the epistle stands the
emphatic statement, spoken with full apostolic authority:
"I exhort you."[1] But Paul exhorts those who have experienced God's mercy. This mercy must become operative in
man's action and the continuing mercy of God will make
human action possible in the future.

The exhortation is first of all an exhortation to sacrifice.
Sacrifice is the primeval word and deed of religion. The
gospel does not dissolve but fulfills. There is no relation to

God without the earnestness of sacrifice. Nothing of that is left out in the New Testament. But the sacrifice has become something new. It is above all the sense of the sacrifice which is new. Idolatry may think that the sacrifice is to be performed in order to win over the demonically angry God and thereby obtain his favor and his gift. According to the gospel, however, God's mercy always precedes. The community has already experienced it abundantly. The sacrifice can now only be an offering of thanks. The object of the sacrifice is also new. Man does not offer a piece of his property but his body, his life, himself. And naturally not only in the inwardness of preparedness but also corporally in action determined by obedience. The sacrifice is no dead gift such as an animal which is killed. Rather it means and demands being there with one's whole life for God. The sacrifice is holy for it is singled out of the world, given over to God, accepted by him and taken into his domain. (On this meaning of holy, see under 1:7.) It is a sacrifice truly pleasing to God; not like the sacrifices of the disobedient people in the old covenant which the prophet must refuse in behalf of God (Is 1:11ff: "What care I for the number of your sacrifices? says the Lord. I have enough of wholeburnt rams and fat of fatlings . . . learn to do good") but rather (Ps 51:19): "My sacrifice, O God, is a contrite spirit." This is true worship and true worship can only be spiritual.[2]

True sacrifice and true worship by the Christian is the Christian life. To Paul this cannot mean that the Church would not also have a public liturgical worship service. For Paul himself speaks forcibly of the celebration of the eucharist (1 Cor 10:11). But this certainly means that this worship is hypocritical if one's life does not correspond to it. It also bears out Jesus' saying that one cannot sacrifice on the altar if one is living in discord with one's brother (Mt 5:23).

(12:2) As the sacrificed one the Christian is removed from this world and belongs to another, new and future world. The Christian is redeemed from the present world (Gal 1:4: "Christ sacrificed himself for our sins, that he might deliver us from this present wicked world"). But as always man must also make God's gift his own. The Christian may not let himself be formed according to the style of the old world which is gone, but must form himself according to the style of the new world (so also 6:4). He must transform himself through that renewal of the mind which cannot be done once and for all but must take place unceasingly. The renewal must take place, however, according to the word and will of God which are declared and are always declared anew to the Christian. In each new situation the Christian must ask himself what the will of God is for him at this moment and thereby what is good, pleasing to God and perfect. Christian life is always new decision in obedience to the God who challenges man altogether personally at every instant. Every Christian stands personally before God and he cannot ultimately leave the decision to others—to a Church, for example, conceived as an authority. Rather he has the right and the honor to live in a direct relationship to God and thereby, of course, the duty to bear up to the direct relationship and to obey.

Wherein the holy living sacrifice is to consist, what is to proceed from the renewal of the mind, what is the good and the perfect which the will of God ever demands (12:1f)—this will now be presented individually in the exhortation 12:3—15:13.

(12:3) The Christian must understand every gift which he has received as a duty for service to the community. Paul derives his exhortations from this principle. (So is it also the word of the Lord that every higher calling means more profound service: Mt 20:26; 23:11.) Paul exhorts to moderation. Since this is the first in the series of exhortations and since Paul declares it with emphatic reference to his apostolic commission, and since he directs the admonition to every individual in the community, it must have been especially urgent and directed toward a particular phenomenon in the community. Perhaps enthusiasm and ecstasy were over-esteemed in Rome as in Corinth (1 Cor 12:14). Perhaps certain gifted persons assumed a superiority over others or thought themselves to be above faithfulness in little things or above the order of the community. Paul does not want to extinguish spiritual endowment (1 Thess 5:19) but he exhorts to prudence and judgment. Moderation is found in the demand for self-discipline and community order—it is what is fitting, "sensible" and "prudent." Another limitation is the measure of faith God has given to each one (so also Eph 4:7). The measure of faith is for each one the measure of his life. His task is apportioned according to the strength of his faith. Each one has received his gift—and he has certainly received it abundantly, because God is abundant toward

all (10:12)—but the endowment is manifold in kind and
significance. Each one's grace is each one's freedom because
it is each one's responsibility before the God who gives.

(12:4f) Paul explains the necessity of moderation and
order with the image of the body and its members, which
in all their diversity make up a unity.[3] The many believers
together form the one Church. It is as inconceivably
wondrous as the complex organism of a body. All are
members of this body whose life and spirit is Christ. Truly
Christ is present in the world and in time through the
Church, his Body. With this image of the body Paul makes
it graphic and clear that the individual members of the
Church have different gifts and duties but that all form
a unity in being for and with one another.

(12:6) The teaching following from the image is applied to the reality of the Church and then immediately to
individual cases. As in 1 Cor 12:8–11 (there even more
fully) Paul enumerates, in a series of seven outstanding
examples, the gifts of grace and of the Spirit which are
operative in the Church. All of them together form the
abundance and fullness of the one Church.

Paul mentions first of all prophecy. Prophecy in the
sense of the Old and New Testaments is not only the
prediction of future events. Rather prophecy literally means
simply announcement and so means that guiding, exhort-
ing, consoling and healing utterance published to the community as God's instruction. For this reason there are
prophets not only in the Old Testament but also in the
New Testament where they are often mentioned as the
spiritually endowed teachers of the Church. The prophet

knows that he is called by the Spirit and speaks out of
the Spirit. This could lead to errors and confusions if a
prophet spoke not out of genuine inspiration but in false
fanaticism, appeared as a virtuoso of enthusiasm, or ven-
tured upon questions to which his faith was not equal.
Prophecy must therefore be practiced "in harmony with
faith," that is to say, it is only genuine insofar as it springs
from the true strength of one's faith. Let the prophet thus
conduct himself within his calling, which is then genuine
if it serves the community. If he disrupts the community
he is misusing his gift. That this could happen becomes
clear from 1 Cor 12:10; 14:29, although here a special
test of the authenticity of prophecy is demanded.

(12:7) He who performs services—be it through word
or through deed toward those in need of help (15:25,31;
2 Cor 8:4)—let him perform his service according to calling and mission. The same applies to the teacher. His service in the Church was certainly above all the interpretation
of the Old Testament Bible and the explanatory transmission of the apostolic tradition of the New Testament
which, of course, was at first not yet set down in writing
in the gospels. Of such a teacher Jesus says that he should
be a true head of a household who brings forth from his
store new things and old (Mt 13:52). Thus Paul also wants
to exhort the teacher to serve the transmitted word and
not his own opinion.

(12:8) As a special gift Paul mentions consoling in admonition and admonishing in consolation. Whoever has
received this gift should give to others out of it. Whoever
dispenses alms—Paul must be thinking of the charity al-

ready practiced publicly by the Church at that time—let
him do so in a modest and selfless simplicity which is completely devoted to the need of the other, and wants to do
nothing but help. Whoever occupies the office of administration of the community or has a share in the administration, let him do it with devotion and zeal. The New
Testament must already know of peevish officials if the
apostles have to exhort the priests to carry out their charge
cheerfully (1 Pet 5:2). Whoever shows mercy, let him
do it with joyfulness. Here again Paul probably does not
so much mean private, benevolent dispensing of charity—
it certainly holds true that God loves a joyful giver (2 Cor
9:7)—but rather community services like care of the poor
and sick. Whoever is entrusted with these services, let him
do them with personal sympathy and joyful visage, not
with bureaucratic mien and hearty indifference. In the
world an office may mean power, in the Church it is service. All her offices must be performed according to the word
of her Lord: "You know that the distinguished rulers of
the Gentiles lord it over their subjects, and that their
princes tyrannize over them. But that is not your way! On
the contrary, he who would be a prince among you must
be your servant, and he who would be a leader among you
must be the slave of everyone" (Mk 10:43f).

(12:9) If in 12:3–8 Paul spoke of individual services
so now in 12:9–21 he deals with the basic attitudes of
Christian life which all must realize, and especially with
the one service which is everyone's duty and which must
be done in great diversity: the service of love. Paul joins
the sentences together in a series of aphorisms with no

strict linking together of ideas discernible. But it is certainly not by chance that the exhortation to love stands at the beginning (12:9a). It is the fulfillment of the law (13:10) and everything else follows from this basic direction of life. Among the further maxims there are three in which Paul warns against the power of evil (12:9b, 17,21). Thus love, as the good, and evil struggle with one another.

Love must be true. It must not be simulated (literally: it must not be an act) as is also admonished in 2 Cor 6:6; 1 Pet 1:22. Who does not know how often the word love is misused! Is it really true that it is merely "the most beautiful form of selfishness?" There is love which does not seek itself but rather the good of the other. If it is not possible on man's part then it is possible as the love which springs from God (1 Jn 4:7). An aphorism with two opposite members further demands at the beginning of the series a fundamental decision between good and evil (12:9b). The Christian must cling to the good as the man to his wife (Gen 2:24).

(12:10) Love should be particularly strong toward one's brothers (on this title, see under 1:13), thus as solicitude and kindness in the Christian community. Paul characterizes it as sincere and solicitous love, like the love which unites the members of a family. (One is reminded that, although not expressly elsewhere in the New Testament yet in the prayers of the Roman Missal, the Church is often characterized as a family.) In the bond of love, however, if it is to endure, there must also be the distance of respect. He who loves should consider and respect the other more highly than himself. This can take place in a sincere way because the other is always that brother to whom God subordinates me for service. Thus the other stands always above me.

(12:11) As of the administrators (12:8) so of all is zeal demanded. The apostle certainly does not wish over-industriousness, but indifference in the community is just as impossible in this tension-charged time in which the return of the Lord is urgently near (13:11). In the face of demanding tasks no one may sluggishly tarry. Paul is hardly thinking of human enthusiasm but rather of the consuming fire of spiritual endowment springing from God when he later admonishes: "Be inflamed in the spirit." As almost always in the New Testament the word spirit here must mean not the natural spirit of man but rather the divine Holy Spirit.

(12:11c, 12a) The two phrases: "Serve the age[4]—Rejoice in hope" seem to be associated with one another. They complement one another in that they contrast present and future. That the Christian should serve the age does not mean that he is to accommodate himself to circumstances, or perhaps even follow the masses and the fashion. Rather the Christian should recognize in what the decisive hour demands, the demand of God, and strive to fulfill it. In this sense the motto can hold good: *Vox temporis vox Dei.* Out of the demanding and perhaps oppressive present the expectation of hope turns toward the future. Hope is not vague optimism but certainty which trusts in the word of God and has already received the beginning of the consummation (5:2–5). For this reason hope is constant reason for and source of joy.

(12:12b) Confident hope gives the strength for per-
severance and endurance under all burdensome oppression
(5:3). The Christian's endurance does not aspire to the
grandeur (or pose) of tragic heroism. Rather the Christian
knows that his capacity derives from the strength of God
in human weakness (2 Cor 12:9). For this reason the
Church holds out in distress in prayer, in which she looks
forward to her future and holds fast to God as the guarantee
of the future. Just as Paul himself prays unceasingly so he
himself exhorts to unremitting prayer (Eph 6:18; Col 4:2;
1 Thess 5:17). Also the two parts of the sentence 12:12b
are thus intrinsically bound together just as distress and
prayer belong together.

(12:13) The two exhortations—to share in the distress
of the saints and to practice hospitality—again form a pair
since both demand assistance to brothers in faith. For once
again (as in 1:7) the saints are one's fellow Christians. In
all external needs and difficulties Christians must offer
mutual support to one another. A form of assistance often
necessary is hospitality to Christians who are on journeys.
If, with the lack of sufficient guesthouses in antiquity,
hospitality was in general a necessity this was also and
especially true among Christians. Messengers were often
under way between communities and they were to be
lodged as brothers. Or ill will, already beginning here and
there on the part of pagans, forced Christians to abandon
their former location. They also tried at first to find ac-
commodation elsewhere with their brothers in the faith.
Arriving Christians had certainly to be welcomed especially
often in the community of the metropolis of Rome. It is

therefore understandable if in the New Testament epistles
the admonition to practice hospitality often recurs (1 Tim
3:2; Tit 1:8; Hebr 13:2; 1 Pet 4:9). But one should not
just submit to the necessity unwillingly (1 Pet 4:9: "Show
ungrudging hospitality to one another"). Thus Paul exhorts
also to eager practice of hospitality. One must not only
practice politeness from a sense of duty; rather love must
be fulfilled toward strangers and the homeless.

(12:14) From the Church the gaze turns outwards in
12:14 and further in 12:17–21 toward those who face individual Christians or the whole community as strangers
or enemies. The commandment of love (12:9) is valid not
only within the community but toward everyone. Love must
also become love of one's enemies. Christians must bring
forth the blessing of God also to their enemies with their
wishes and prayers. That man can bring about blessing is
in Israel pious confidence, out of which comes the custom
of the blessing. Thus Jacob blesses his children (Gen
48:15; 49:25f), the priest the people (Num 6:22–27), the
godly man the godly (Ps 23:4f). Also and above all Christians, who have received the fullness of the blessing, must
pass it on (15:29).

But in Israel the curse is also practiced—the calling
down of temporal and eternal damnation on the enemies
of God and of Israel (thus Moses' curse, Dt 27:14–26; 30:7;
the psalms of malediction, 108:6–20; 118:21; 136:7–9).
It is a new covenant when Paul twice demands blessing but
forbids every curse. For the God of the new covenant is
the Father of all, of both the good and the evil (Mt 5:45).
Paul's commandment and prohibition are similar to the

saying of Jesus (Lk 6:28): "Bless those that curse you."
Other apostles likewise say that cursing is impossible for
Christians (James 3:9–12; 1 Pet 2:23; 3:9).

(12:15) The exhortations refer again to conditions in
the community, whereby they lay down basic attitudes.
The demand to be joyful with those who rejoice and to
weep with those who weep requires being there in the
preparedness of one's whole person for the others, with
one's will as well as one's heart.

(12:16) As in every community so also in the Christian
community there must have been differences of opinion
for objective or personal reasons. But Paul demands here
as elsewhere (1 Cor 1:10; 2 Cor 13:11; Phil 2:2; 4:2) that
quarreling and dissensions be overcome. To fulfill the demand "to agree in thought with one another" absolutely
and in all things is hardly possible, however. Paul thus
demands that unity be reached in essential matters of the
community. Or perhaps Paul is referring to special difficulties of some Christian communities (cf. 1 Cor 4:10;
2 Cor 11:19). Perhaps he is hinting that some who thought
they had received special graces or sublime revelations of
the Spirit had assumed a superiority above the everyday
life of the community, whose unassuming matters and
services seemed too lowly to them. They were in danger of
breaking off from the community and going their own, as
they thought, more sublime spiritual ways. Paul asks them
also to respect what is unpretentious and not to consider
themselves wise. Paul demands the courage to serve the
humble through humility.

(12:17a) As in 12:14 Paul speaks further in 12:17–21 about conduct toward non-Christians. Verses 12:17f take up once more the commandment to love one's enemy (12:14). A double commandment to do good (12:17b, 18) corresponds to the prohibition against repaying evil with evil (12:17a). The negation is swallowed up in the positive, the evil in the good. Room must not be given to evil even in self-defense (1 Thess 5:15).

(12:17b, 18) Rather it is a question of being intent on what is good and noble toward all men; and for this reason also of being prepared for peace with all. Jesus himself blesses those who make peace (Mt 5:9) and keep peace (Mk 9:50). Paul repeats this exhortation (2 Cor 13:11; 1 Thess 5:13). Here in 12:18 he must, it is true, twice limit his demand as if with sorrowful resignation: "If it be possible, as far as lies in your power."

Paul must not be thinking merely or principally of the relation of person to person but of the Church in relation to her environment and to the world. The Church is of course, with regard to the world, fundamentally ready for peace. She will not provoke dissension on her own. But in many respects she stands in opposition to the world and this opposition can some day break out hostilely. And the Church can be forced into opposition and battle for the sake of her mission.

(12:19) The verses 12:19–21 deal further with conduct toward hostilely disposed non-Christians. Once again the exhortations begin negatively (12:19a) only to close with positive declarations. They are so important to the apostle that in closing he proves and strengthens them with several passages from the Old Testament word of God (12:19b, 20).

The Christian may be forced to defend himself yet even so the intention and desire for revenge are forbidden him. Should he want to avenge himself he would pretend to the rights of God, to whom alone judgment belongs. But what can God's revenge be other than his love? The Christian must therefore place his own conduct under the commandment and the risk of the love of his enemy.

(12:20) What the Christian himself can and may do is overcome the enemy through love. Paul expresses this— with no concern about a possible misunderstanding—by using a very graphic and drastic saying from the sapiential literature (Prov 25:21f). In these Old Testament proverbs an almost banal and self-seeking shrewdness sometimes expresses itself. Of this sort is also the advice to overcome the enemy with good deeds. They will be for him as unbearable as glowing coals on his head. He will be ashamed and will change his conduct.

(12:21) The sense of the admonition of 12:20, as well as of the whole section 12:17–21, is summed up as if with a maxim. In the eternal cycle of revenge evil always generates evil anew. Thus evil gains the overwhelming predominance in the world. The Christian must break open this cycle of disaster and make a new start with the good. And Christians together must reverse the relation of good and evil, help the good to predominate and bring about its victory.

2   THE CHRISTIAN IN THE WORLD

13: 1–14

13: 1 Let everyone submit himself to the ruling authorities, for there exists no authority not ordained by God. And that which exists has been constituted by God.

   2 Therefore he who opposes such authority resists the ordinance of God, and they that resist bring condemnation on themselves.

   3 Rulers are not a source of fear in regard to good actions, but only in regard to evil ones. You wish, then, not to fear the authority? Do what is good and you will have praise from him.

   4 For he is God's minister for your benefit. But if you do evil, fear, for not without reason does he wear the sword. He is God's minister, an avenger to inflict punishment on evildoers.

   5 Accordingly we must needs submit, not only out of fear of punishment, but also for conscience' sake.

   6 This is why you pay tribute, for they are public ministers of God, devoting their energies to this very thing.

   7 Render to all men their due: tribute to whom tribute is due; taxes to whom taxes are due; respect to whom respect is due; honor to whom honor is due.

   8 Let there be no unpaid debt except the debt of mutual love, because he who loves his neighbor has fulfilled the Law.

   9 For the commandments:
>   "You shall not commit adultery;
>   You shall not kill;
>   You shall not steal;
>   You shall not covet" (Ex 20:13–17; Dt 5:17–21;

and if there is any other commandment, all are summed up in this saying,

> "You shall love your neighbor as yourself"
> (Lev 19:18).

10 Love does no evil to a neighbor. Love, therefore, is the complete fulfillment of the Law.

11 And this do with due regard for the time, for it is now the hour for you to rise from sleep, because now our salvation is nearer than when we came to believe.

12 This night is far advanced; the day is at hand. Let us, therefore, lay aside the deeds prompted by darkness, and put on the armor of light.

13 Let us conduct ourselves becomingly as in the day, not in revelry and drunkenness, not in debauchery and wantonness, not in strife and jealousy.

14 But put on the Lord Jesus Christ, and take no thought for your lower nature to satisfy its lusts.

In Rom 12–15 Paul wants to present the conduct of the Christian in the Church and in the world. The exhortations cannot be strictly divided according to these two respects yet in Romans 13 the relation to the world is especially prominent. And therein an instruction on the attitude of the Christian to the state must not be lacking. For precisely here an important and often distressing question poses itself for the Church. We recognize how important it is from the completeness of its treatment (13:1–7). The way in which it poses itself and in which sense it is to be handled become clear from the fact that Paul takes it up after he has spoken of the attitude toward the heathen, hostilely disposed environment (12:14–21). In fact the relation between the Church community, the civil public and the state authority had almost necessarily to be strained, even unfriendly from the very beginning. Strangers were able to see in the Church nothing but a Jewish sect.

Jewry, separated from the milieu with its own religion and its own customs, was suspicious to many, even hated. Thus there was already in the old world of that time, especially in Rome, an intense hatred of the Jews among certain elements. The Church had to bear her share of the rejection of Jewry. Especially heathen officials might have been tempted to carry their antipathy against the Jews over to the Christians. The Church herself was derived from Jewry. Earnest and devout Jewry's attitude toward the Roman state was often one of rejection, even hostility. There were zealots who in incessant opposition and in continually renewed disturbances tried to impair the Roman government in Israel or to drive it out. Would Christians not also be influenced by it? In addition the Church knows of the kingdom of God, as yet hidden, and expects its speedy public establishment. This could lead to misunderstandings and rebellion against the authority of the state. The question of the state and the Christian community could thus be in many respects grave and difficult. For this reason it is understandable that it is repeatedly treated in the New Testament (besides Rom 13:1–7, also Mt 22:15–22 and synoptic parallels; 1 Tim 2:1f; Tit 3:1; 1 Pet 2:13–16; Apoc 13).

In verses 13:1–7 Paul speaks in general of the state and of every state. But he is not thinking of some ideal state but of the one which really exists. In the Mediterranean world of that time this is the Roman empire. In Corinth where Paul is writing the epistle it is represented by the office of the proconsul. And the recipients of the epistle in Rome refer the admonitions, and obviously should refer them, to the imperial state. Moreover Paul is not thinking primarily of fundamental and theoretical questions; rather he wants to give concrete, practical instruction which goes as far as the attitude of the Christians toward the tax collector.

(13:1) The Christian stands vis-à-vis the state in an obligation of obedience which is grounded in faith. For the state is as divine an order as is the order of creation, a fact which Paul establishes emphatically with a doubled "by God." Thus when the Christian acknowledges the state and its officials he does not obey men but God.

(13:2) But then rebellion against the state is rebellion against God's order and God himself. It will therefore fall under God's judgment. A penalty inflicted by the state against opposition is not merely a reaction of the state's authority toward the law breaker but the punishment of God which reaches the disobedient man by means of human agency.

(13:3) There is therefore no reason for a rebellion. There is only one logical possibility of conflict with the state: the misdemeanor or crime. Whoever fulfills the law has nothing to fear from the state. He will even receive the approval of the authorities.

(13:4) If the state is founded and supported by God's will it can thus actually be called God's minister. It serves God's order in that it protects the good and punishes the evil. For this reason the state has penal authority, even for the death penalty.[5] By means of this penal authority divine anger over the injustice intervenes in human reality, and behind the human instrument the divine will to justice becomes visible.

(13:5) Obedience toward the state and its authority must be performed not only out of fear of the disciplinary authority and the punishment of the state but out of the conviction of one's conscience (on the term and concept of the conscience, see under 2:15).

(13:6) The duty of obedience includes the special and altogether concrete duty of paying one's taxes. For this reason it applies precisely to financial officials in that they are officials of God.

(13:7) The acknowledgement of the state must thus take place externally and legally through payment of taxes and tributes, but also in the inner attitude of fear and honor.

Paul's words recall Jesus' explanation of the question of liability to taxation with reference to a coin: "Therefore render to Caesar what is Caesar's and to God what is God's" (Mt 22: 21). The similarity seems so great that exegesis considers it possible that Paul knew this saying of the Lord and that it is the basis of the Pauline demand and formulation.

Paul's words on the attitude of the Christian to the state are exceptionally moderate. They acknowledge reality and exhort one to adapt oneself to it. Yet these words are astonishingly without reservation. According to 13:2–4 it seems to be absolutely certain that the rightdoers have only good to look forward to from the state; whereas the evildoers, and only they, have to expect the rightful punishment.

Yet Paul certainly knows what Jesus Christ suffered from the Roman governor and from Roman administration of justice. And what did Paul himself experience from the Roman authorities! In Philippi they had him and his companion Silas flogged and thrown into prison (Acts 16:22f). The "imprisonments and lashings" which Paul mentions in 2 Cor 11:23 probably refer to the exercise of authority that he experienced on the part of the Jews as well as the Romans. According to Rom 8:35 he is prepared for the worst, death by the sword, which only Rome could carry out. For an understanding of Paul's teaching it is to be remembered that there was a broad and deep stream of tradition of a Jewish theology of creation and of history which recognized and taught that God is the Lord of kings and nations who raises up political authorities and lets them sink again. Thus Isaias (45:1) can call the Persian king Cyrus the anointed one of God. At the time of the New Testament honorable sacrifices were regularly offered for the emperor and the empire in the temple in Jerusalem. Accordingly Paul can also speak of Rome with such great appreciation. But it must not be overlooked that in verses 13:1–7 the limitations of the state are also shown by implication. That the state is the minister of God (13:4, 7) not only confers its right and its authority but also its limitation. It is not an autonomous lord, so that everything is right which is profitable to it; rather it is the minister of another. It must represent the order established by God. Will it not lose its authority of command and regulation if it violates that higher ordinance? Further: the state is conscious of God's will to judgment and anger. Yet God's will is not merely will to angry judgment but will to salvation. It is not the state but the Church which effects God's will to salvation in the world. The state is not God's minister for the entire will of God but only for a part. Thus the task of the state is also limited here. After all Rom 13:1–7 is not all that Paul has to say about the state. In the epistle to the Church in Philippi (3:20) he explains: "As for us, our commonwealth is in heaven, and it is from there that we eagerly await our Savior, the Lord Jesus Christ." The Christian is thus actually a citizen not of the earthly but of another state, where his salvation is being prepared. For an evaluation of present-day questions concerning the relation of state, church and Christian it should not be forgotten that the Roman empire at the time of the New Testament, and thus Paul's "state," knew only of the subject's obligations toward the state but of no mutual responsibility of the citizen in and for the state, and of no obligation to cooperation resulting therefrom. Here the Christian is charged with an obligation today which did not exist in the state of that time.

(13:8) Proceeding from 13:1–7, where he has dealt with the fulfillment of the obligations and debts to the state and its officials, Paul comes to the obligations among men in general (13:8–10). Paul thinks first of all of legal obligations. The Christian does not deem them unimportant. Love may go beyond the law but it does not disregard it. One can fulfill legal obligations in such a way that one is no longer indebted. Yet one can never fulfill love so as to be quit. One always owes love not only because it is practiced ever imperfectly but because the will to love a person is a never-ending movement. But it is nevertheless true that even if one always owes love one may never rest content with the fact that one always owes it. Rather one must always practice love as if one could fulfill it. With this love the true, essential and entire demand of God's law—given in the Old Testament but valid forever—is fulfilled.

(13:9) In the commandment to love one's neighbor all the separate commandments of the Ten Commandments are fulfilled.[6] The separate cases are only an application of the general commandment of love. Paul's teaching is like that of Christ himself in that the whole law and the teachings of the prophets hinge on the one commandment of love of God and of one's neighbor (Mt 7:12; 22; 39f).

(13:10) In another respect it again follows that all commandments are contained in the commandment of love. The various commandments are intended to hinder us from doing evil to our neighbor. But love only wants to do him good and is consequently the antithesis of the desire to do him evil. The various commandments thus put into practice in each individual case the all-inclusive attitude of love. And love fulfills all commandments.

(13:11) In verses 13:11–14, at the close of the general exhortations, Paul gives another reason which is important to him: the Lord is coming soon! That makes the exertion for the life of faith extremely urgent. The Church must always be ready to receive her Lord.

For this reason it is now necessary to awaken from sleep and to rise. The image[7] is easily understandable; sleep is the state of moral indifference, waking that of moral striving. But the salvation now urgently near is, as gradually becomes clear from the following words, not primarily the salvation of the individual soul or of the entrance into bliss which takes place with death, but the day of salvation for the entire creation. The universe will be gloriously renewed when with the return of Christ at the end of time God's dominion and kingdom are established (so also Hebr 9:28; 1 Pet 1:5). This day is for Paul as for the recipients of the epistle nearer now than when they came to believe. This is in itself something self-evident, just as it can be said of every event and day lying in the future. Paul does not want to state something so obvious. He evidently wants to say something else, something very urgent. The day he means is not a far-off day which will perhaps occur in millenniums but rather a very imminent day. The Epistle to the Romans may have been written in the year 57–58. Most of the Christians therefore have been practicing the faith for only 20 to 25 years or less. But this short span of time has decisively brought the day of the Lord's return a great deal closer. Paul is clearly not counting on millenniums until the return of the Lord but on a short, a very short space of time. Our conclusion from his words is confirmed by further declarations of the New Testament. Other statements of Paul (Phil 4:5; 1 Thess 4:15–17) as well as of the gospels (Mt 24:29; Mk 9:1; 13:28–30) attest that the Church of the apostles counted on the possibility of a quick return of Christ, and indeed hoped and longed for it.

(13:12) A new image of night and day continues the related one of sleeping and waking (13:11). Night is an image of the old age that still continues; day signifies the longingly awaited, newly dawning age of salvation. At the same time night and day represent evil and good, for evil seeks the protection of the night whereas good can show itself openly in the day. As Paul writes this epistle the age of night has advanced almost to dawn. The sun can shine up over the horizon at any moment. This means, without imagery: at any moment Christ can appear in his glory. Even if the night of waiting is not yet over, the works of the day must nevertheless be accomplished.[8] Otherwise there is the danger that he who is still doing the deeds of night will be surprised by the suddenly dawning day.

(13:13) The light of day demands honesty and discipline of life. Licentiousness and wickedness are becoming to night and hide themselves in it. In a short catalog of vices (see under 1:29–31) Paul does not enumerate vices of his own choosing but portrays and condemns the life of pleasure; in other words the social decadence in a Graeco-Roman city. Paul himself must have occasionally seen and heard such occurrences.[9]

(13:14) With and according to the renunciation of the dissolute life the faithful are to put on Christ.[10] This expression means that the Christian in the sacramental event of baptism has died and risen with Christ and must now act and live in the manner and spirit of Christ (Rom 6). Opposed as another possibility to this Christian life is the life of the flesh, that is, lust, sin and death. Therein must the Christian not be subservient.

Paul admonishes in anticipation of the arrival of the Lord, just as the Church of his time lived in this anticipation. In all her hope for the imminent consummation the Church nevertheless knew that for man the day of the Lord's return was hidden and God's way withheld and could not perhaps take place for yet a long time (Mt 28:19; Mk 13:32,35; 1 Thess 5:1f; 2 Thess 2:1f). Finally the Church had to recognize that God, before whom a day is like a thousand years and a thousand years like a day (2 Pet 3:8), has other measures of time than human calculation. But just as in Rom 13:11–14, the New Testament continually says that judgment and consummation are not only something that will take place in some far-off time but that faith in the face of the approaching advent of judgment and salvation always lives in the certainty and anticipation of the consummation. In the New Testament the Church is thus directed toward her future, which comes from God, and in this anticipation she gains the true perspective toward all things: "This I declare, brothers, that the allotted time has become very short. From now on those who have wives should live as though they had none, and those who weep should be as though they were not weeping, and those who rejoice should be as though they were not rejoicing, and those who buy as though they had nothing, and those who make use of this world should live in such a way as not to become engrossed in that use, because the stage setting of this world is passing away" (1 Cor 7:29–31).

3 STRONG AND WEAK
IN THE ONE CHURCH

14: 1–23

14: 1 Welcome among yourselves the person who has a weak
conscience, but avoid disputes about opinions.

2 One person's conscience says that he may eat anything,
but he who has a weak conscience eats only vegetables.

3 He that eats should not despise him that eats not, and
he that eats not should not condemn him that eats, since
God has welcomed this latter one into his household.

4 Who are you to condemn another's household servant?
It is his master's concern whether he stands or falls; and
he will stand, for God can keep him standing.

5 Another prefers this day to that; still another puts all
days on the same level. Let everyone have his own complete mental conviction.

6 He who has a mind to observe the day, does so for the
Lord's sake; and he who eats does so for the Lord's sake,
since he gives thanks to the Lord. So too he who does
not eat, abstains for the Lord's sake, and gives thanks to
God.

7 None of us lives for himself, and none dies for himself.

8 If we live, we live for the Lord, and if we die, we die for
the Lord. Whether we live or whether we die, we are
the Lord's.

9 To this end Christ died and lived, that he might be Lord
both of the dead and of the living.

10 But you, why do you condemn your brother? Or why do
you despise your brother? We shall all stand before the
judgment seat of God.

11 So it is written,
"As I live, says the Lord,
to me every knee shall bend,

and every tongue shall give praise
to God" (Is 45:23).

12 Therefore everyone will render account of himself to God.

13 Let us then no longer judge one another, but rather resolve not to put an occasion of sin or a stumbling block in your brother's way.

14 I know and I am fully convinced in the Lord Jesus that nothing is of itself unclean; but to him who regards something as unclean, it is unclean.

15 If then your brother is upset because of what you eat, no longer do you act according to the demands of love. Do not with what you eat destroy him for whom Christ died.

16 Let not then your privilege be reviled.

17 For the kingdom of God does not consist in food and drink, but in holiness and peace and joy in the Holy Spirit.

18 He who in this way serves Christ pleases God and is approved by men.

19 Let us, then, pursue the things that make for peace and mutual edification.

20 Do not for the sake of food destroy God's work! All food is certainly clean, but food is evil for man who eats it while giving in to bad example.

21 It is good not to eat meat and not to drink wine, nor to do anything by which your brother is offended or induced to sin or weakened.

22 You have a conscientious conviction: Keep it to yourself before God. Blessed is he who does not condemn himself by his own decision.

23 But he who eats when he is in doubt, condemns himself because his act does not come from conscientious conviction; for every act that does not proceed from conscientious conviction is sinful.

In the Church of Rome there was a minority of the "weak" which was despised by the majority of the "strong." Paul is writing for the recipients of the epistle who were acquainted with the situation. But he does not express himself precisely enough for the sources and the circumstances of the dissension to be positively discernible in each case to us today. The weak abstain from partaking of meat (14:2,21) and of wine (14:21) for to them these foods are "unclean" (14:14). They observe special days of the week (14:5), thus, certainly, special holidays and fast days. Since pious Jewry observed numerous days it is likely that these scrupulous ascetics were Jewish proselytes (according to the tradition of the ancient Church James, the brother of the Lord and the first bishop of Jerusalem, as a strict penitent partook of neither meat nor wine). The Church in Rome from its very inception certainly had ties to the Jewish community there (see introduction above, page 18). Since, however, the Jews abstained from pork but not from meat in general the weak had perhaps been influenced by other abstinence movements which had long existed at that time even among the Gentiles.[11]

The Christians stemming from the Gentile peoples considered themselves free even of Old Testament food ordinances (like the prohibition of pork), and understood still much less that stricter abstinence. The Jewish Christians were offended by this freedom of the Gentile Christians while the Gentile Christians despised the constraint of the Jewish Christians. Each group isolated itself from the other. The community of faith and the unity of love were endangered.

All these details and circumstances may be things of the past but it must remain normative for the Church how

Paul, in his settlement of the dissension that had arisen, protects both things: the unity of the Church and the freedom in the Church. The principles and admonitions by means of which Paul provides a solution can perhaps be summed up as follows: do not judge but let it pass! (14:1–12). Do not give offense but be considerate! (14: 13–23). But above all the example of Christ! (15:1–13).

(14:1) The apostle turns first to the strong, who predominate in the community in number and kind. And he demands from them: "Welcome among yourselves the person who has a weak conscience!" The weak person also has the right to be in the community. One must not thereby pester the dissenter with quarrels and judge his opinions and convictions or drive him out of the community or exclude him.

Paul's instructions must not be misunderstood. He is surely not the man who avoided decisions and put up with everything for the sake of peace. He demands the testing and distinction of members (1 Cor 12:10); he reprimands and calls to account (1 Cor 4:18–21; 2 Cor 10:2). If he perceives ruinous influences he separates the community from them at all costs and excludes members inexorably: thus the unchaste man (1 Cor 5:6–13) or false teachers (2 Cor 10:2; Gal 1:8). In such cases the verdict can only be: "Expel the wicked man from your midst" (Dt 17:7—1 Cor 5:13).

But in the Roman community it is evidently a question of other things. The differences of views mentioned in the Epistle to the Romans seem to us considerable (especially to us who experience various kinds of centralism with its elimination of opposition). But for Paul they are not so important that they could be a reason for separation. Paul himself does not share the conviction of the weak; he himself belongs to the strong (15:1). But in the Church one must be able to tolerate and allow other views. Christians must welcome and support one another just as "Christ has cordially welcomed you to himself" (15:7), and as God welcomes, supports and tolerates all of us with all our imperfections and weaknesses (15:3). Paul, reflecting and meditating on the transmitted gospels in sermons and epistles, has performed a great labor of thought from which the Church lives until this day. He certainly does not want to restrain thinking and discussion. But he does forbid quarreling over opinions if violence and injustice thereby occur and the fraternal community suffers injury. In particular the Church must have patience with her scrupulous brothers who only want to follow their consciences with complete earnest. Even when a conscience errs while seeking God's sanctification one may not forcibly upset it.

(14:2) At other times Paul severely opposes those who pronounced ascetic customs or legal practices current among the Jewish people as necessary for salvation and who therefore wanted to impose them upon all Christians. For Paul this is a false trust in works and is not founded on grace. For this reason it also loses grace (Gal 5:4f). Such an asceticism seems to be penance and piety yet it is only wilfulness and fulfillment of fleshly desires (Col 2:23). Against such temptations Paul rigorously defends the freedom of Christians. But it is not a question of that in Rome. One also may not impute such conclusions to those "weak in faith"[12] and thereby slander them. For this reason the Christians in Rome who hold differing opinions can and must retain their freedom.

(14:3) The strong man who eats everything without scruple is tempted to despise the weak man because he supposes that the latter, as a little mind, lacks freedom and independence. The strong man does not understand that the restraint of the weak man is a point of obedience which merits respect. But too the weak man may not judge and condemn the strong man. He judges, perhaps, that the freedom of the strong man is lack of self-discipline, earnestness and desire for sanctification. In his pious self-restraint the weak man does not understand that freedom is not self-liberation but freedom given by God. He forgets that God has welcomed the unconstrained man as such. When God has passed his judgment no man may condemn. The abstinent man as well as the unconstrained man lives by God's grace.

(14:4) Paul further protects the strong man from condemnation by the weak. God has welcomed the strong man into the household as a household servant. The unconstrained man is responsible to his Lord alone and is withdrawn from the judgment of the weak man. The statement of the apostle applies first of all to the case of the strong and the weak in Rome but fundamentally to every man. This means that every believer stands finally before God in the directness of his conscience, into which no one may intrude.

Paul describes the legal condition of the slave as a standing and falling before his master. He is not speaking of a usual master-slave relationship but of the relation of man to God. And here he does not want to leave the statement, that man stands or falls, unprotected. Man is certainly always in the moment of decision between standing and falling, between standing the test and falling into sin. But he is not alone in this danger and not given up to just himself or to fate, but rather he is in God's love. For this reason Paul appends an emphatic addition: man does not fall. He will stand for God is able to keep him standing.

(14:5) The two groups of the community differentiate themselves with regard to the selection and observance of certain days. The pious Jew fasts two days of the week (Lk 18:12). Did the weak also consider themselves obliged to keep such fasts, perhaps in addition to other days of fast— Wednesday and Friday, for example, which were already observed in the first century in remembrance of the passion of Jesus (cf. Mk 2:20)? Or did they think they still had to observe the Sabbath, perhaps in addition to Sunday, which already in the apostolic Church replaced the Sabbath as the holyday (Apoc 1:10)? Paul does not want to enforce any uniformity in such matters. He evidently considers this both unnecessary and inadmissible. Here every man can and should "have his own complete mental conviction." There can be a diversity of human opinion in the Church that one must not reduce to uniformity. This holds good without detriment to the fact that the Church must be composed in the unity of the Spirit (1 Cor 12:13; Eph 4:4). But multiplicity of human thinking does not exclude unity of the Spirit.

(14:6) The statement of verse 14:3b is supplemented.

If there it was stated that it is the individual relation to God, so now it is also the relation to Christ which is decisive. Both the weak man and the strong man want to be obedient to Christ in their way. He who keeps the fast days does so to please Christ. The strong man who eats without fasting does so in obedience to Christ. One can perceive this from the fact that the strong man, like the weak, gives thanks to God when he eats. If the strong man partakes of food with gratitude to God he receives it as God's gift and in the conviction that he has the freedom of eating. But also the weak man who deprives himself when he eats takes his nourishment with gratitude to God. Both give thanks because both want to honor God in conscientious and joyful obedience. Perhaps Paul recalls the saying of grace in common, because precisely at the meal which the Christians often celebrated in fraternal community (according to the evidence of Acts 2:46; 1 Cor 11:17–34) differences of views became painfully evident. But according to the conviction of the apostle the intimate eating community must be able to put up with and span even such nonetheless important differences. The fact that a common discipline and asceticism are enforced does not make up the unity of the Church, but the fact that she acknowledges God in one faith and belongs to him in one obedience does.

(14:7f) Every man stands in the responsibility of his own conscience but at the same time all undisciplined arbitrariness is excluded. Every conscience and every life has its strict order in the bond to the Lord. The disciple

belongs to his Lord Christ in his entire life and beyond
life.

(14:9) Christ has acquired his lordship over the Church
through his work of salvation. In the suffering of death he
has ransomed the Church from the slavery of sin and the
devil and in the strength of his resurrection she herself has
risen to life. His salvation is the hope and life of the faithful in death as in life.

With verses 14:7–9 Paul wants to confirm his assertion
that the Christian, whether he fasts or eats, considers himself
bound to the one Lord. But in content these verses go far
beyond what is necessary for proof for they speak of the
community of Christians with the Lord in life and in death.
The sentences are thereby composed as if in rhythms and
stanzas. As in a solemn creed and hymn they revolve around
the words live and die. The statements on the living and
dying of Christians are linked in artistic parallelism with
those on the death and life of Christ in that the fate of
the Christian and of Christ are related to one another. The
verses 14:7–9 are further set off from the context by the
fact that they are formulated in the first person plural
whereas the preceding and following sentences are description or address. From all this one is probably to conclude:
Paul seems to take over a text as a whole and to insert it
into his epistle. Does he perhaps have a baptismal hymn
in mind and want to remind his readers of it? The Christians experienced baptism as dying and rising again with
Christ (6:3–11). We may assume such an origin for 14:
7–9 so much the more when Paul, for example, also in
Eps 5:14 reminds the Church of a baptismal hymn:

> "Thus it is said,
>   Awake, sleeper,
>   And arise from the dead,
>   And Christ will give you light."

And in 2 Tim 2:11f a baptismal confession seems to be cited:

> "Trustworthy is the saying,
>   If we have died with him,
>   we shall also live with him.
>   If we endure,
>   we shall also reign with him."

All of these epistle passages are solemnly and rhythmically formulated in the same way. All deal with mysterious dying and living. All of them may come from the ancient ceremony of baptism. Such ancient fragments of the liturgy of the Church are extremely precious to us.

(14:10–12) After Paul has shown that Christ is the Lord of all he repeats the assertion, now more profoundly established, that every Christian is responsible to this, his Lord alone, and directly to him, and for this reason is withdrawn from every human judgment. The sentence of the judgment of this Lord will alone decide. Paul confirms this forcibly and conclusively with a saying of Scripture which he models after Is 45:23, i.e. with a word of God, which finally settles all quarreling among men.

(14:13) With verses 14:13–23 Paul turns principally to the strong, whose conduct is especially important in the given circumstances for the preservation of the unity of the community. (And this always holds good in like manner!) The weak cannot follow the strong. They would violate the bond of their conscience, even if it is not free from error. But he who is strong can certainly for the sake of the weak renounce using his freedom inconsiderately.

Verse 14:13 ensues and infers from verses 14:10–12: judging and remonstrating others is not permitted to the Christian. But he must align himself toward what is right. This demands that no one may become a stumbling block and downfall for others. Who is a stumbling block for whom? Perhaps he who is weak to the community if he burdens it with his overly great scrupulousness. But still more he who is strong, if he should embitter the weak man through his lack of consideration or prevail upon him and provoke him to acts which would conflict with his conscience and take from him security and peace, or which would even be sin for him. The weak brother must be respected and supported in his weakness. But all must show consideration.

(14:14) Paul himself renounces freedom. He stands on the side of the strong. He gives reasons for this, his conviction, by referring to the Lord Jesus Christ with whom he knows he is in agreement. It seems that he wants to refer to a saying of the Lord similar to the one which the gospels have preserved (Mt 15:11): "Not what goes into the mouth defiles a person, but what comes out of the mouth is the thing that defiles a person."[13] Certainly all of the ordinances of the Old Testament law about defilement by certain foods or procedures were abolished with this saying of Christ. According to this saying there could be no more defilement and sin through external things. Certainly pure and impure still apply to Christians, but they are no longer

differentiated by an external law but by one's personal
conscience before God. The conscience is henceforth the
binding law of the Christian. The religion of law is overcome by the religion of conscience. This of course in such
a way that in the case in question the weak man is bound
to his conscience even if it is erroneous.

(14:15) The conscience of the other, thus the scrupulous conscience of the weak brother, is protected. Paul reproaches the strong brother with the result of his lack of
consideration. Even what is in itself harmless and permitted
becomes in this way injustice. If he who is weak sees the
strong man eat he is offended and sad. Whoever is in-
different about this is acting contrary to love. The weak
man can finally become so embittered that he separates
himself from the community. Or perhaps he lets himself
be misled against his conscience to imitate the strong man
and becomes guilty. For the sake of a trifle like food the
brother is destroyed. Paul places the antithesis before our
eyes: Christ died for the brother. He who is strong wants
to have lust for his food, whereas Christ gave up his life
for the other. He brings death through what he considers
life, whereas Christ brought life through his death. With
his frivolity he turns against Christ himself.

(14:16) The sense of the exhortation, "Let not then
your privilege be reviled," is not to be positively determined.
Who is it who reviles and what is it that is reviled? Do
non-Christians who learn of the quarrel in the community
on this account revile the Church and the gospel she
preaches? Or is Paul turning to the strong in order to ad-

monish them not to abandon their noble blessings of freedom to misunderstanding and slander?

(14:17) In Paul as in the entire New Testament God's
dominion and kingdom are blessings which will be revealed
in complete reality and consummation after the end of the
present age. Yet they begin right now even if they are so
far only present invisibly. Col 1:13 already holds good: "He
has rescued us from the power of darkness and transferred
us into the kingdom of his beloved Son." But God's kingdom is not present here and now in the fact that the Christian may eat and drink what he wants; rather it is present
there, where holiness, peace and joy are wrought by the
Holy Spirit. For it is these blessings which make up the
future kingdom of God. In the sanctification given by God
the sanctified will then live in the presence of God and in
blissful peace with one another. The future kingdom must
now come into being symbolically in the community of the
Church. Divisions between the strong and the weak would
be the antithesis of this. They are unjust mutual condemnation instead of sanctification, dissension instead of peace,
sorrow instead of joy (14:15).

(14:18) Paul intensifies the admonition by reminding
the Christian of his responsibility toward the Lord (cf. further 15:1–13). Christ has secured holiness, peace and joy for
the Church through his service and he secures these blessings
for her forever. In the following of this Lord the Christian
must embody these same values. All morality must prove
its authenticity in two respects. It must fulfill God's commandment and order and it must serve the human com-

munity. Whoever promotes justice, peace and joy surely meets both demands.

(14:19) Out of all this Paul finally comes to the exhortation to build up the community in peace with all one's strength. Without peace it is not possible to build up a community.

(14:20) The opposite of building up would be tearing down. Thus the work of God, which is the Church established and created by him and beyond that the whole work of salvation, would be destroyed by divisions in the Church. This must certainly not happen on account of such a trifling thing as food. It is true that Paul repeats the fundamental statement that all legality has been overcome (14:14). Everything, as God's creation, is good and pure and the proper use of all things is left to the conscience. But precisely for this reason the good becomes evil for him who uses the good with a bad conscience. This would occur if he who is weak ate with bewildered conscience— or even if he believed that he would thereby violate God's sacred commandment.

(14:21) For this reason Paul finally lays down with apostolic authority the principle: better to have nothing from all that than to give offense to one's brother. If the concern for one's brother demands it the Christian must relinquish his freedom and his right.

(14:22) A closing word is addressed to the strong. No one must give up his conviction. He who is strong need not renounce his conviction that he has the right of freedom. Rather he should be certain of it before God. But he must perhaps give up demonstrating his freedom before his

brother so as not to offend him. The confirmation of his
conviction by God is sufficient. It does not need confirmation by men. Let he who is strong see to it that the right
which he grants to himself is not self-deception. May it
also be granted to him in God's judgment. It is before this
judgment that man must stand steadfast, not before his
own. If the Christian is thus referred to his conscience
this does not mean freedom as caprice but rather the
strictest obligation.

(14:23) And now a word to the weak. If he who is weak
is unsure in his judgment and still acts, then he is already
condemned. He ignores the admonition of his conscience.
He has thereby fundamentally given up obedience to God.
Thus Paul finally lays down the principle: "Every act that
does not proceed from conscientious conviction is sinful."
Whoever acts contrary to knowledge and conviction—even
if it is an erroneous conviction—is condemned. But for
Paul conviction is never merely profane understanding but
always associated with and determined by religious faith.
Paul demands man's fidelity to himself in unconditional
desire for obedience to God. All man's thinking and action
is decision between unbelief and belief. It is either a Godless act or else it comes from life's profound foundation,
from faith, and is responsibly performed therein. There is
no third possibility.

The views and questions which divided the strong and
the weak in Rome belong to the past. But other questions
now threaten or split the unity of the Church. The re-
flections and principles developed by the apostle are still
valid for their evaluation and final conquest. Are there not

always the weak in the Church, such as those who are unenlightenedly scrupulous or those who want to limit freedom out of zeal for the law? The strong must support the weak and put up with their backwardness. But they must also respect the obligation of conscience of the weak, which is earnest desire for obedience. God's act of salvation is intended for all men, even the weak. Christ died also for them. God's plan of salvation is also effective among them. He who is strong must not endanger the work of salvation. Rather a greater responsibility is imposed upon more profound understanding and refined faith. If he who is strong became a stumbling block for the weak by asserting his understanding and his right, then he would have to relinquish them. Perhaps "we, the strong" consider various sects and confessions as such weak brothers. The apostle would forbid the Church to separate herself from them with arrogant judgment and to exclude them. They are and remain brothers.

4 ABOVE ALL: THE EXAMPLE OF CHRIST

15: 1–13

15: 1 We, the strong, ought to bear the infirmities of the weak, and not please ourselves.

    2 Let everyone of us please his neighbor, doing him good by edifying him,

    3 since Christ did not please himself, but as it is written,
        "The reproaches of those who reproach you
        have fallen upon me" (Ps 68:10).

    4 For whatever has been written beforehand, has been

written for our instruction, that through the patient endurance and consolation afforded by the Scriptures we
may have hope.

5 May then the God who imparts patience and comfort
grant you this unity of sentiments among yourselves according to Jesus Christ,

6 that, one in spirit, you may in a harmonious chorus
glorify the God and Father of our Lord Jesus Christ.

7 Therefore, welcome one another cordially, even as Christ
has cordially welcomed you to himself for the glory of
God.

8 I declare as a matter of fact that Christ Jesus has been a
minister of the circumcised to show God's fidelity in
realizing the promises made to our fathers,

9 while the Gentiles glorify God because of his mercy,
as it is written,

"There shall I praise you among the Gentiles
And shall sing to your name" (Ps 17:50).

10 And again the Scripture says,

"Rejoice, you Gentiles, with his people" (Dt
32:43).

11 And again,

"Praise the Lord, all you Gentiles;
and sing his praises, all you peoples" (Ps 116:1).

12 And again Isaias says,

"There shall be the root of Jesse,
and he who arises to rule the Gentiles . . .
in him the Gentiles shall hope" (Is 11:1, 10).

13 May God, the source of hope, fill you with all joy and
peace based on faith, that you may abound in hope by
the power of the Holy Spirit.

Verses 15:1–13 conclude the discussion on the faction
of the strong and the weak in Rome. The previous
considerations are thereby deepened. Paul raises the particular case of the Romans to a principle and speaks in
general of the strong and the weak in a community. The

widening of significance seems to be reflected also in the change of style. Paul no longer speaks of those weak in conscience as opposed to the strong, but in general of the "feeble," the "weak," as opposed to the "strong" (15:1). But then the exhortations are newly and forcefully confirmed in that Paul refers to the example of Christ, who became the servant of all (15:3,5–8), and verifies the exhortations with sayings from the Old Testament Scripture (15:3,9–12). The present moment is thus clarified out of the depth of Old Testament history and of the eternal redemptive action of God. And it is his principle to judge the random present in reference to the eternal Christ.

(15:1) While Paul considers himself to be among the strong, he acknowledges their real, superior right only, it is true, to speak immediately of their duties. Superiority is not the right to rule over others but the duty to serve. For he who is strong is capable of supporting. Thus the strong in the Church must support the weak; not merely put up with them, which could be an attitude of arrogance, but serve them as those to whom all the same rights in the community are acknowledged. The opposite would be for the strong man to live to please himself; that is, to do without consideration what he thinks proper. Perhaps he believes he is thereby serving the cause and the right but he is only serving himself.

(15:2) Everyone must embody the opposite, namely, pleasing his neighbor. This does not mean feeble complaisance toward others but what Paul immediately demands: help each one that he may grow in good and that thus the whole community be edified.

(15:3) How this is to take place is presented, as an example and an obligation, by the ideal life of Christ portrayed by the verse Ps 68:10. Christ did not think of himself and his right. Rather he renounced everything. He even gave up his honor and his life in order to take upon himself in exchange the abuse and the scorn with which the godless wanted to revile God himself. Christ was able to say of himself: "The reproaches of those who reproach you have fallen upon me."

Ps 68 is the pious man's lamenting prayer of petition uttered out of profound abandonment and distress. But he who is praying is convinced that if the godly man is abused it is really intended for God himself, to whom he belongs. The just man and the sufferer thus intercepts in his suffering the opposition against God. Paul sees the figure of the worshipper in Ps 68 renewed and fulfilled in the Christ of the passion. In Ps 68:22 it says that the enemies give the just man gall and vinegar to drink. It was precisely what the crucified Christ suffered (Mt 27:34,48). And he took upon himself the abuses of the godless Jews, who reviled him on the cross: "He trusts in God: let God deliver him" (Mt 27:43). Thus in the face of the Crucified One it was called into question whether God is he who is capable of saving his own from distress. Christ on the cross bore the slanderous doubts which were intended for God. Ps 68 is used over and over again in the New Testament in this way in order to describe Christ's way to the cross, his suffering and his death (Lk 12:50; Jn 2:17; 15:25; Acts 1:20; Rom 11:9f). The great psalm of suffering (Ps 21) is similarly applied (Mt 27:35,39,43,46; Jn 19:24,28), several verses of which clearly refer to the crucified Christ; thus Ps 21:17: "They have pierced my hands and my feet" and 21:19: "They divide my garments among them, and for my vesture they cast lots." When the apostles and the Christians of the apostolic Church read such psalms, deeply moved, they saw them fulfilled almost verse for verse in the figure of the suffering and dying Lord. In the interpretation of Scripture, in meditation and in preaching they explained the Old Testament texts in the light of the life of Christ. To them he was the Most Righteous One and the Saint of God who gathered up in himself all the godly men of antiquity. Everywhere, in ancient times as in their own, they perceived one and the same work of salvation of God. In this interpretation of the Old Testament—that the passage refers to Christ—which appears so many times in the New Testament, we see into the heart of the Church, which belongs to her Lord, Jesus Christ, in faith, prayer and love.

(15:4) Paul inserts a fundamental consideration of the interpretation of Holy Scripture (i.e. of the Old Testament) in the Church. According to it nothing of what is reported in Scripture is reported only to relate the history of an earlier age. Rather everything which is there recorded is written down for the instruction, exhortation and consolation of the later generations in the Church. Especially the many examples of endurance, patience and fidelity (as of the just man oppressed by suffering in Pss 21 and 68) are to be for the latter a strengthening for their own patient endurance. The many tales of God's help are to be faith's promise and guarantee that God helps even now.

The faithful should derive consolation therefrom, stand fast in the face of all obstacles in hope and confidence and be certain of God's care.

(15:5) The consideration of verse 15:4 is followed by a wish in the form of a prayer. The Scripture is able to secure patience and comfort because it is full of God, who is the God of patience and comfort. May he produce and give to the Church the blessings which are contained in the Scripture. Paul applies this wish to the situation of the Roman Church. May God comfort the community by restoring the unity and harmony between the two groups. This should take place according to the example of Christ and in conformity with his Spirit (15:3).

(15:6) The unity should and will declare itself then in the unanimous glorification of God and of the Lord Jesus Christ.[14] If God is only One then only that glorification can be genuine which comes from a Church united in love. A Church which is split in dissension and strife cannot worthily and fittingly fulfill her mission of acknowledging God with praise. The saying of the Lord (Mt 5:23f) finally applies to the Roman community as to the entire Church: "Suppose, then, you are about to offer your gift at the altar, and there remember that your brother holds something against you: leave your gift there before the altar, and first go and settle your argument with your brother; and then come back to offer your gift." Should it not seem to us that the separated Christian communities stand under the word of the Lord and the admonition of Paul?

(15:7) Paul confirms his exhortation anew with a reference to the life and work of Christ. The separated groups must be willing to acknowledge one another as legitimate, to welcome and receive one another mutually. Both must leave their seclusion and begin to come together. The great example for that is the act of Christ. He has created the Church as one in that he welcomed both Jews and Gentiles. He did this to the honor of God. The Church must certainly not diminish or destroy this honor. Again and again in his epistles Paul wants to praise the fact that Christ brought Jews and Gentiles together in one Church as the overflowing abundance of God's act of salvation (cf. for example, Rom 10:12; 1 Cor 12:13; Gal 3:28; Eph 2:14–22; Col 3:11).

(15:8) Christ welcomed the Jews in that he became a minister of the circumcised; that is, he submitted himself to the law of Israel. God had promised the Messiah and the salvation of the redemption to Israel's forefathers and his entire chosen people. Christ entered into the people of Israel so that these promises of God would find their fulfillment and the truth and fidelity of his word would be revealed.

(15:9–12) Paul describes how Christ also brought God's mercy to the Gentiles in that he joins together four Old Testament quotes which speak prophetically of the future rejoicing of the peoples over their redemption. Since the Gentiles are entering the Church they can really praise God in this way. David (Ps 17:50) already began to sing the jubilation among the Gentiles (15:9). Moses (Dt 32:43) called upon them to rejoice together with God's chosen people (15:10). Again Ps 116:1 summons all peoples, thus Jews and Gentiles, to praise God (15:11) and Is

11:1,10 prophesied that the sprout from the root of Jesse[15] would also rule prosperously over the Gentile peoples (15:12).

(15:13) Having come to a division of the epistle Paul concludes with solemn praise of God and prayer. The words and concepts taken from the Old and New Testaments which describe salvation are joined together as in a precious chain: hope, joy, peace, faith, power and Spirit. God is the God of hope. He has revealed the future through his word and he guarantees this future through his veracity and fidelity. As an advance gift of the future salvation he already gives the Church joy and peace now. But they are imparted in faith, that is, in the individual human decision and act which is faith. And may God—this is the wish of the apostle—give the overflowing abundance of hope in the power of the Holy Spirit. The Spirit of God is to disclose hope to the Church and strengthen her in hope. Thus Paul mentions two possibilities and ways to experience grace: faith as a personal act and the Spirit as the power of God. The two do not exist independent of one another but in mutual permeation.

FOOTNOTES TO CHAPTER V

¹ The Greek word can be translated implore, console or exhort. In Paul's usage the entire content of the word is spoken and heard. To exhort, on the other hand, is neither to command nor to abuse.

² With the term "the worship of mind and soul" Paul takes up an idea and a word formation of the philosophical religion of the Greeks of his time who recognized in their most noble intellects that to a spiritual God only spiritual sacrifices of man, and not animal sacrifices, can be suitable and pleasing. Paul has probably not taken the formula from Greek philosophy itself but through transmission of the Jewry of his time, which was influenced by Greek culture; similarly 1 Pet 2:5.

³ The image was often used in Graeco-Roman antiquity. The tale is well known of how Menenius Agrippa, with the fable of the limbs which no longer wanted to obey the body, induced the element of the citizens of Rome which was isolating itself on the Sacred Mountain to return to the city. Paul also uses the image in 1 Cor 12:12–27 where it is enlarged upon in detail; further in Col 1:18–24 and Eph 1:23; 4:16; 5:23, where he more fully develops and deepens the theology of the Church as the body of Christ.

⁴ It is questionable which text Paul wrote. Some of the manuscripts give the text "Serve the age," others "Serve the Lord." The exhortation "Serve the age" is more unusual than the more familiar "Serve the Lord." Since it is always more likely that the unusual is replaced by the usual than vice versa, the reading "Serve the age" seems to be the genuine and ancient wording.

⁵ That the state wears the sword (i.e. the executioner's sword as the symbol of authority over life and death) may be meant not only figuratively but also actually, for the highest officials in Rome had the fasces with the axe—and in the provinces the sword—

carried around before them as a sign of the power over life and death.

⁶ Departing from our practice the Ten Commandments are enumerated in the order: adultery, murder, theft, covetousness, thus the sixth, fifth, seventh, ninth, and tenth commandments. The commandments are thus ordered, however, in some of the most ancient Hebrew and Greek manuscripts of the Old Testament.

⁷ The image is obvious and is often used both without and within the New Testament; compare Mt 24:24f; 25:13; Lk 12:37; Acts 20:31; 1 Cor 16:13; Eph 5:14; Col 4:2; 1 Thess 5:5–10; 1 Pet 5:8; Apoc 3:2f; 16:15.

⁸ The good works are accomplished with the weapons of light. These weapons of the struggle of Christian life are depicted in detail in Eph 6:14–18. The imagery is not seldomly used outside of the New Testament; thus in the recently found scrolls of Qumran, one of which, called "War of the Sons of Light with the Sons of Darkness," portrays in detail the battle of the good and the evil and their armaments. The image lives on when we speak of the "Church militant."

⁹ As Augustine (Confessions 8:12), at the request of the children: "Take and read," opened the New Testament, his eye fell, as you know, on Rom 13:13. The words unnerved him so much, because he found therein the everyday life of the aristocratic Roman portrayed.

¹⁰ The image may ring unfamiliar to us but it is not uncommon in biblical usage. According to the Old Testament man can put on holiness as well as sin (Ps 108:28f; Job 29:14; Wisd 5:18). The New Testament says that the Christian puts on Christ (Gal 3:27) or the new self (Col 3:10; Eph 4:24). Does a recollection of baptism play a role here, since the baptismal candidate laid aside his old garment on stepping down into the baptismal well, and received a new, white robe on climbing up once more?

¹¹ Diogenes Laertius (8:38), a writer of the third century A.D., says of the neo-Pythagoreans, who also had a community in Rome: "They eat vegetables and drink water with them."

¹² When Paul uses the word faith in 14:2 it is evidently not in the sense of saving faith, but merely a simple belief or opinion [and thus, in English, conscience—tr].

¹³ That saying of the Lord is also cited in Acts 10:15; 11:9 in order to solve the question of whether the Old Testament dietary laws are still valid. Thus it was considered by the Church as the authoritative instruction of Christ, with which she justified the fact that she no longer observed the Old Testament law.

¹⁴ The designation or more accurately the glorification of God as "God and Father of our Lord Jesus Christ" recurs often in the New Testament (2 Cor 1:3; 11:31; Eph 1:3; 1 Pet 1:3). It seems to be a hymnal and liturgical prayer formula of the New Testament. God is the God of Christ in the eternal source of the Son. He is the Father in the eternal union of love between Father and Son.

¹⁵ David's father was Jesse (or Isai). The Messiah is the son of David, and thus he is a descendant of Jesse or "a sprout from the root of Jesse."

VI CONCLUSION

15:14—16:27

The concluding section of the epistle contains, as in other Pauline epistles, personal communications about the missionary labors and plans of the apostle, references to individual situations in the community, blessings and greetings. The conclusion of the Epistle to the Romans thereby corresponds in many ways to the introduction (1:8–17). Here as there it is stated: Paul has the firm intention to come to Rome (1:10 and 15:22–24, 28f, 32). As apostle to the Gentiles he is obliged also to the Roman community (1:5f, 14–16 and 15:15f). The apostle is bound to the community in prayer (1:9f and 15:30–33). With his visit he wants to secure for the Roman Church a share in the grace and the blessing of Christ (1:11–13 and 15:29) and, of course, also be strengthened himself by her (1:12 and 15:24). These personal communications in the introduction and in the conclusion preserve in the comprehensive document, dogmatic and didactic throughout long sections, the style of a real letter.

1 PLANS OF THE APOSTLE

15: 14–33

15:14 I myself, my brothers, am convinced in your regard that you too are full of goodness, replete with all knowledge, so that you are able to admonish one another.

15 Yet I have written to you rather boldly here and there, brothers—as it were to refresh your memory—

16 because of the commission given me by God, to be a public minister of Christ Jesus to the Gentiles, performing priestly functions by means of God's gospel, that the oblation of the Gentiles may become acceptable, being sanctified by the Holy Spirit.

17 I have, therefore, this boast in Christ Jesus as regards the work of God.

18 I do not make bold to mention anything but what Christ has wrought through me to bring about the conversion of the Gentiles, by word and deed,

19 with mighty signs and wonders, by the power of the Holy Spirit, so that from Jerusalem, and that in all directions, as far as Illyricum, I have fully preached the gospel of Christ.

20 But I have made it a point of honor not to preach the gospel where Christ has already been proclaimed, lest I build on another man's foundation.

21 But as it is written,

"They who have not been told of him shall see,
and they who have not heard shall understand" (Is 52:15).

22 This is why I have been hindered these many times from coming to you.

23 But now, having no further field of action in these parts, and having had for many years a great desire to visit you,

24 when I set out for Spain I hope to see you as I pass

through and to be sped on my way by you, after I have to some extent satisfied my desire for your company.

25 At the moment, however, I am setting out for Jerusalem to bring help to the saints.

26 For Macedonia and Achaia have thought it well to contribute to the needs of the poor among the saints of Jerusalem.

27 Such has been the good pleasure of the former, who have thus made the latter their debtors. For if the Gentiles have shared in the Jew's spiritual blessings, they should also aid their Jewish brothers with material blessings.

28 So, when I have completed this task, and have turned the proceeds over to them, I will set out by way of your city for Spain.

29 I know that when I come to you, I shall come with the fullness of Christ's blessing.

30 I beseech you, brothers, through our Lord Jesus Christ, and through the love of the Spirit, that you struggle with me in prayers to God for me,

31 that I may be delivered from the unbelievers in Judea, and that the proffered help may be acceptable to the saints at Jerusalem;

32 that I may come to you in joy, by the will of God, and may enjoy some rest with you.

33 May the God of peace be with you all. Amen.

In verses 15:14–18, Paul establishes how and why he has written to the Roman Church. If the knowledge of being the founder and father of a community bestows the right of instruction and exhortation vis-à-vis other communities this is not the case between Paul and Rome. Is he here meddling in other people's affairs? For this reason Paul explains and justifies his epistle with winning politeness.

(15:14) Paul knows that the Roman Christians possess

virtue and knowledge in rich abundance. They do not need his exhortation, but are capable of finding the proper words of order and admonition and of taking the necessary measures. According to this statement of Paul a community itself is charged with the service of mutual admonition and ministerial work. It is not only the duty of the official clergyman. Paul does not want to infringe upon this autonomy of the community.

(15:15) With fraternal amiability Paul admits that he has written rather boldly. It was bold for him to write to a strange community at all. And it was bold when he at times admonished with such forcible earnestness. But he can maintain that he has actually taught and demanded nothing but only recalled what holds good everywhere in the Church. And he has only done what he had to do out of the grace of his calling. For grace is always also responsibility.

(15:16) The service of the apostle is at bottom priestly ministry. Paul is not merely a teacher and educator of the Church but carries out the preaching of the gospel as priestly service. He sacrifices with the community, and sacrifices himself in its offering (Phil 2:17: "But even if I am made a libation upon the sacrificial offering which is your faith, I am glad and rejoice with you"). He is called to prepare peoples and the world so that they become offerings sanctified in the Spirit before God. The sanctification takes place both through the word and sacrament of the Church and through the faith of Christians. In few passages of his epistle does Paul let us get such a profound insight into his consciousness of vocation. He considers

himself a consecrated priest who stands as a mediator between the world and God and offers the peoples to God
as a sacred sacrifice.[1]

(15:17) Paul must suspect that one considers such a
consciousness of vocation of the apostle all too lofty. But
he is not boasting of himself and he is not important to
himself. He can only boast of Christ and only the work of
God may be important to him. Before the world the apostle
is only "the world's scum, the scapegoat of society" (1 Cor
4:13).

(15:18) But thus through him Christ's salvation is
wrought on the world. Paul knows that everything which
he has said Christ has wrought through him so that the
Gentile peoples may attain faith (1:5; 6:17). Paul describes
his missionary labor as happening by word and deed. God's
Spirit is mighty in both. Christ praised the apostles (Lk
10:23): "Happy are the eyes that see what you are seeing,
and the ears that hear what you are hearing." Thus Paul
also accomplishes the missionary work by preaching and
signs. He calls the latter signs the wonders and the power
of the Holy Spirit. He may understand by these terms the
sacramental signs and the act of worship in which God's
working remains hidden beneath the sign. But for him it is
unquestionably certain that he also has at his disposal the
power to perform visible miraculous signs (2 Cor 12:12).
He hardly speaks of this for he has only Christ to proclaim
and not his own deeds (2 Cor 11:18; 12:1). Yet the Acts
of the Apostles and the missionary history of the Church
(such as in Mk 16:17f; Hebr 2:4), tell of the signs and
wonders which accompany the preaching of the apostles.

In word as in deed God works salvation. This will always be valid for the character of the Church. She is not only the Church of the word but also the Church of the sacrament.

(15:19) Paul has done his missionary work in this power of God. Thus has he been able to lay a fiery circle of the gospel over the lands from Jerusalem as far as Illyricum, from the east to the west. He has proclaimed the gospel in this whole wide expanse. He has traveled through these lands repeatedly and there, abiding for shorter or longer periods, he has brought the gospel to full strength. To be sure small communities exist only in a few cities. Nevertheless Paul says that the preaching of the gospel is completed there. He is convinced that the message, once it is kindled, will progress and spread out from the middle point in an irresistible conflagration and that the mighty word will not come to rest until it has conquered everything. The expectations of the apostle turned out to be correct. Already in his time we learn of Christian communities in Colossae and Laodicea, cities in which Paul never stayed but where churches founded by missionaries from Ephesus arose. A short while later the first Epistle of Peter (1:1) goes out to the churches in "Pontus, Galatia, Cappadocia, Asia, and Bythinia." And the Apocalypse of John (2 and 3), still before the end of the first century, testifies to communities in Ephesus, Smyrna, Pergamum, Thyatira, Sardis, Philadelphia and Laodicea. So quickly were these great regions won over to the Christian faith by the gospel spreading out under its own power.

(15:20f) On his missionary journeys Paul has the principle and the ambition to always preach only there, where the name of Christ has not yet been proclaimed. To do anything else would seem to him as if he wanted to build on another's foundation, intrude into the rights of others and rob others of their honor. Thus a prophetic saying (Is 52: 15) to be fulfilled in his work says that the messenger of God will come where the message is still unknown, and will be understood where one has not yet heard anything about it.

(15:22f) Yet now Paul wants to come to Rome. He has long had this intention. The responsibility of the great duties of the mission prevented him until now from carrying out the plan of journeying to Rome. But he was able to complete his work in the east and now he will come to Rome.

(15:24) Yet according to his principle of not building on another's foundation (15:20) Paul does not want to stay long in Rome. He intends only to stop there on the way to Spain. Yet he would like at least to get to know personally the Roman community, famous throughout the entire world (1:8). Paul indicates his conviction that he will be sped on his way from Rome, thus that the Roman Church will sustain his long journey.[2] Paul knows that he will find refreshment and strengthening in the Roman community even if, as he almost jokingly says, the short stay will not suffice to satisfy him completely (cf. 1:12).

(15:25) Before the journey to Rome Paul wants to fulfill still another urgent obligation. He must travel first to Jerusalem in order to deliver there a collection of money which was decided on by the Church in Macedonia and Achaia. The Church of Jerusalem is called the "community of saints." If Christians in general are designated as the saints (1:7), the original community in Jerusalem seems to have called itself the community of saints in a special sense (15:31; 1 Cor 16:1; 2 Cor 8:4; 9:1,12); they designated themselves thereby (after Ex 19:6; Lev 11:44f) as the elect of the end of time. Perhaps the title "the saints" ("the holy") has gradually been transferred from the community in Jerusalem to the other Christians.

(15:26) The Church in Jerusalem also calls itself "the community of the poor."[3] This not primarily on account of poverty in money and property; rather it is the poor in spirit, oppressed by the unjust and brutal, who stand under God's special protection.

(15:27) The Gentile Christian communities have decided on the collection for Jerusalem as an expression of community. The collection is not an imposed tax but a voluntary testimony of the bond that exists between them (15:26). On the other hand it is also the liquidation of a debt, as Paul also states. The Gentile Christian communities are indebted to the mother church in Jerusalem. Thence have they received the spiritual gifts of the gospel and it is just and reasonable that they give thanks for that with earthly goods.

Not so much the Epistle to the Romans but all the more so do the other epistles of Paul reveal that he had to undergo a great deal of opposition from the Jews of Jerusalem, but also from the unenlightened Jewish Christians there. Paul acknowledged the primary election of Israel and their lasting honor on that account (1:16). But the Jews persecuted him because he maintained that after Israel had

rejected her Messiah the Gentiles had entered into the
election. There were narrow-minded Jewish Christians who
accused him of no longer recognizing the binding force of
the Old Testament law for the Church (Acts 21:21).
Paul's opponents followed him into his missionary regions
and often enough he had to defend and protect the communities, which he had founded with great difficulty in the
freedom of the gospel, against the attacks of his opponents,
who tried to degrade the apostle personally and who demanded of all Christians the additional observance of the
Old Testament Jewish law. In spite of everything Paul does
not want to forget, and the Gentile Christians must not
forget, that the gospel went out from Jerusalem into the
world and all peoples are therefore greatly indebted to the
original community in Jerusalem. This applies not only to
the Church in Paul's time but also to the Church and the
Christian world forever, and it would even apply to a completely secularized world (Jn 4:22): "Salvation comes from
the Jews."

(15:28f) Paul first wants to "seal" the fruit of Christian
love, that is, conclude the collection and deliver it in
Jerusalem. Then he will come to Rome on his journey to
Spain. He knows that he will bring to the community the
fullness of the grace and the blessing of Christ (1:1).
Similarly he assures the Corinthians that his visit will bring
them grace (2 Cor 1:15). Paul does not boast of his own
abundance and capability of dispensing grace. He knows that
he is desperately poor but also, of course, that he can make
many people rich; that he has nothing but possesses everything (2 Cor 6:10). He comes as Christ's apostle, in the

commission of Christ and therefore with his fullness of blessing. He conveys it to the Church. Once again (as in 15:16) his priestly consciousness expresses itself.

(15:30) Paul looks forward to his journey to Jerusalem with anxious and uneasy presentiments (15:30–33).[4] If he asks the communities for their intercession (2 Cor 1:11; Eph 6:19; Phil 1:19; Col 4:3,18; Philemon 22) so especially in this situation. He asks the Christians in Rome for their prayers with reference to the fact that both community and apostle serve under one Lord and are bound in the one love of the Spirit. Thus all take care of one another. The prayer of the Church is to support the apostle in the struggle. The biblical prototype of the struggle of prayer is the struggle of the patriarch Jacob with the angel of God that lasts from night to dawn (Gen 32:24–30). The expression and image of the struggle of prayer do not mean that anything was to be forced from God which he otherwise did not want to give. The opponent in this struggle is not God but rather the powers hostile to God, which are to be pinned down and overcome with God's help. According to the New Testament Christ has also led the struggle against them. Thus the apostle, the Church, Christ and God stand together in battle.[5]

(15:31) The prayer is to support the apostle in a twofold concern. It is to protect and save him from the hostility of the "disobedient," i.e. of the unbelieving Jews. If the faith, according to Paul, is obedience to God's word (1:5; 15:18) then unbelief is disobedience (2:8; 10:21; 11:30f). With deadly hatred Jewry persecuted Paul as an apostate. The Acts of the Apostles testifies in its account (ch. 21–26) how

well founded the apprehensions of the apostle were. It re-
lates that the persecution of the Jews brought Paul into
imprisonment in Jerusalem and brought his life into extreme danger. But Paul also feared hostility in Jerusalem
from the Jews who had become Christians. Therefore the
prayer of the Roman community is to aid him so that the
collection which he is conveying will be gladly welcomed
and accepted by them. Acts 21:21 speaks of their possible
rejection of Paul since it was rumored among them that
Paul was misleading the Jews to defection from the law (an
accusation which was not completely without foundation,
since he pronounced circumcision and other commandments of the Old Testament law to be obsolete). Yet Paul
certainly respected the pre-eminence and dignity of old
Israel (1:16; 9:1–5) and of Jewish Christianity (15:27),
and he therefore seeks understanding and peace with the
original community in Jerusalem this time too, just as he
did on earlier journeys there (Gal 1:18; 2:1–10).

(15:32) Beyond all these dangers and cares Paul anticipates the future day when he may come to Rome full of
joy, according to the will of God, and find comfort and
rest in the community there. Who would not understand
that the restless wanderer finally longs for this?

(15:33) Paul's deep longing for peace also declares itself
when he wishes it to the Roman community in a blessing.
God is peace and peace is in him. A great harmony encompasses God and the Church in Paul's wish and vision.

Paul's confidence that he would be allowed to come to
Rome in joy and peace was not fulfilled. True, he came

three years later—early in 61—to Rome but not as a free
apostle: rather as prisoner of the emperor (Acts 28:16).

2 GREETINGS AND WISHES

16: 1–24

16: 1 I recommend to you Phoebe, our sister, who is a deaconess of the congregation at Cenchrae,

2 that you may welcome her in the Lord, as becomes
saints, and that you may assist her in whatever business
she may have need of you. She too has assisted many,
including myself.

3 Greet Prisca and Aquila, my helpers in Christ Jesus,

4 who have offered their own neck for my life. To them
not only I but all the congregations of the Gentiles give
thanks.

5 Greet also the congregation that meets in her house.
Greet my beloved Epaenetus, who is the first fruits of
Asia for Christ.

6 Greet Mary who has labored much for you.

7 Greet Andronicus and Junias, my kinsmen and fellow
prisoners, who are distinguished among the apostles, who
also were in Christ before me.

8 Greet Ampliatus, beloved to me in the Lord.

9 Greet Urbanus, our helper in Christ, and my beloved
Stachys.

10 Greet Apelles, approved of Christ. Greet the members
of Aristobulus' household. Greet Herodion, my kinsman.

11 Greet the members of Narcissus' household, who are in
the Lord.

12 Greet Tryphaena and Tryphosa who labor in the Lord.
Greet the beloved Persis who has labored much in the
Lord.

13 Greet Rufus, the elect in the Lord, and his mother, who
has been a mother to me.

14 Greet Asyncritus, Phlegon, Hermas, Patrobas, Hermes, and the brothers who are with them.

15 Greet Philologus and Julia, Nereus and his sister, and Olympias and all the saints who are with them.

16 Greet one another with a holy kiss. All the congregations of Christ greet you.

17 I exhort you, brothers, to watch those who cause dissensions and scandals contrary to the doctrine you have learned; avoid them.

18 Such do not serve Christ our Lord but their own bellies, and by smooth words and flattery deceive the hearts of the simple.

19 Surely your submission to the faith has been published everywhere; I rejoice over you. Yet I would have you wise as to what is good, and guileless as to what is evil.

20 The God of peace will speedily crush Satan under your feet. The grace of our Lord Jesus Christ be with you.

21 Timothy, my fellow laborer, greets you, and Lucius, and Jason, and Sosipater, my kinsmen.

22 I, Tertius, who transcribed this letter greet you in the Lord.

23 Gaius, my host and the host of the whole congregation, greets you. Erastus, the city treasurer, and Quartus, our brother, greet you.

24 The grace of our Lord Jesus Christ be with you all. Amen.[6]

The Epistle to the Romans closes with a long series of greetings (16:1–16) into which is inserted a severe warning against teachers of false doctrines (16:17–20).[7]

(16:1f) Paul requests that Phoebe be welcomed amiably in Rome. Presumably she is to convey Paul's epistle to Rome. The apostle speaks of her with words of high appreciation. She is a sister, thus a Christian (see under 1:13). She has the office of a deaconess in the Church of Cenchrae (near Corinth, where Paul is probably writing the Epistle to the

Romans). She is the only deaconess mentioned in the New Testament. Yet numerous deaconesses are mentioned in the writings of Christian antiquity immediately thereaftei. She has rendered aid and assistance to many, even to the apostle himself. Thus it is just and reasonable that she find the help of the community in Rome. Phoebe must have been an important and respected woman in the apostolic Church. Her Greek name (the pure) marks her no doubt as a Gentile Christian.

(16:3) Paul sends greetings first to Prisca and Aquila, a well to do Jewish couple on very friendly terms with Paul and familiar to us from the New Testament. They had done a lot both for the Church and for Paul himself. Paul had lived in their house on his first stay in Corinth (Acts 18:3). From there they accompanied him to Ephesus (Acts 18: 18). They once "offered their own neck" for Paul, that is, they risked their life for him. Both in Rome (16:5) and in Ephesus (1 Cor 16:19) the Christians gathered in the house of this couple. It is striking that of the two Paul mentions the wife, Prisca, first, just as she is also named first in Acts 18:18,26; 2 Tim 4:19. Was she the more important?

(16:4–15) Also in the following series a remarkable number of women are mentioned and distinguished, moreover, by words of high praise. Mary, no doubt a Jewish Christian, has worked a great deal for the community (16:6). So also the Christian women Tryphaena and Tryphosa and the beloved Persis have labored much in the Lord (16:12). The mother of Rufus has become a mother to Paul himself (16:13). Finally Julia and the sister of

Nereus are also greeted (16:5). One often quotes Paul's instruction in 1 Cor 14:34: "Women are to keep silent at the services." One may obviously not understand this sentence as if Paul did not treasure the service of the woman in the Church. Rather women have rendered highly esteemed assistance in his communities.

Paul mentions several more Christians out of the Roman community. Epaenetus (16:5) is the first fruits of the province of Asia (that is, the region around Ephesus). Thus he was the first to be won for Christ here. Judging from his Greek name he was no doubt a Gentile Christian. The epistle perhaps hints that he had a special place of honor in the community. Andronicus and Junias are kinsmen of Paul (16:7), thus Jewish Christians. They became Christians even before Paul and are thus probably among the oldest members of the original community in Jerusalem. As apostles—messengers and missionaries outside the narrowest circle of the twelve apostles originally received the name apostle—they have performed outstanding services and they have shared an imprisonment with Paul. In verses 16:11,14, 15 Christian households are greeted with their heads or hosts.

Greek, Latin and Jewish names alternate with one another in the list of greetings. A comparison with mentions of names in books and inscriptions from that period shows that the names mentioned by Paul were usually borne by slaves, freedmen and those of higher standing, yet especially, it seems, by the first two groups. Thus what Paul said of the community in Corinth (1 Cor 1:26–29) may have proved true also for that in Rome: "Just consider, brothers,

your own call; not many of you were wise, not many influ-
ential, not many noble by worldly standards . . . what counts
for nought God chose . . . lest any weak mortal should pride
himself in God's sight." Men of the most varied extraction
united themselves together in the Roman community. This
is certainly possible, even probable in a metropolis like
Rome. The Christian faith unites the most diverse men in
a new community (Col 3:11): "Here there is no Gentile,
no Jew, no circumcised, no uncircumcised, no barbarian, no
Scythian, no slave, no free man, but Christ is everything in
each of us."

(16:16) Paul concludes the list with the request for the
holy kiss. In New Testament communities the kiss was a
practice of liturgical worship (1 Cor 16:20; 2 Cor 13:12; 1
Thess 5:26; 1 Pet 5:14). The kiss is holy because it is removed from the otherwise normal use. Perhaps Paul thus
presupposes that his epistle is to be read out in the worship
service and that the reading is then to be concluded with
the liturgical ceremony of the kiss. Paul immediately conveys to the Roman community the greeting of all the congregations of Christ. He can speak in the name of many for
he stands in constant communication with the Churches of
the east by means of messengers and letters. But Paul can
speak thus and in the name of all because of his apostolic
consciousness. The communities are bound to a unity in the
office of the apostle. His word is the word of them all.

(16:17) Between the lists of those greeted (16:3–16)
and of those who send greetings (16:21–23) a severe warning against division of the community by teachers of false
doctrines is surprisingly introduced in verses 16:17–20. As

in the Epistle to the Romans (16:22) Paul no doubt generally dictated his epistles and then added a closing greeting in his own hand; thus 1 Cor 16:21–24; Gal 6:11–18; Col 4:18; 2 Thess 3:17. Rom 16:17–20 also seems to be such a personal signature. Paul had to defend himself in many epistles against false teachers. He is fearful that even in Rome their destructive activity is a possibility or that it may have already begun.

The teachers of false doctrine bring dissensions into the Church and result in seduction and ruin. They have abandoned the transmitted teaching and mislead others to defection. In the Church there exists a transmitted doctrine which is the measure and norm of judgment (6:17). The Roman Christians are to avoid dealings with the false teachers. The apostolic Church discipline demands again and again such a separation from what is false (even in the oldest church regulation Mt 18:17; then 1 Cor 5:9, 2 Thess 3:6; Tit 3:10).

(16:18) Paul's judgment is very severe. False teachers do not serve Christ but their own bellies (the same reproach in Phil 3:19). This does not mean that the false teachers are slaves to crude, carnal vices. Heresy may pretend or even believe that it arises from religious zeal. But it pursues its own wishes and follows its intoxicated spiritual appetites. It does not know the order of moderation and destroys the obedience to the community. It seeks itself, which Paul and the New Testament conceptualization must designate as worldly and carnal and as undisciplined impulsiveness. Paul does not deny the opponents' clever words but rather reproaches them for them. They use highly finished speech and well formed language in order to thereby delude the unsuspecting and the willing. For this reason the apostle's warning is necessary. Precisely when the preaching is proclaimed with the most intense ardor and is heard with self-sacrificing devotion, precisely then is clear-headed examination necessary to distinguish whether the enthusiasm is genuine and true.

(16:19) Paul like all Christians is certainly acquainted with the Roman Church's submission to the faith (1:8). Therefore he does not have to fear that she will fall away from the true teaching (16:17). He wishes and desires that as before, and still more than before, she be wise as to what is good (thus not let herself be seduced to what is wrong with clever words) and separated from what is evil (thus remain preserved from the egoism of the heretics).

(16:20) Paul discloses the sources of all false teaching. Satan is at work in it (cf. 2 Cor 11:14; Gal 1:8). This demands all earnestness of opposition without any coming to terms. Satan wants nothing but confusion and strife. But his adversary, God, is the God of peace. His work of salvation has redeemed the strife of the world. May he give the Church, as he will, the power to overcome all dissension! The victory is described with a mythological image which uses the promise of Gen 3:15: the serpent's head will be trampled under foot. God will force Satan down under the feet of the faithful so that they may trample him. And this will speedily take place. Yet the apostle certainly does not intend merely to affirm that the danger of false teaching will soon be overcome in the Roman community, but rather that the age in which Satan is still permitted his pernicious work will soon elapse. The final consummation is imminent (13:11–13). Paul wishes his community not only the peace of God but also the grace of the Lord Jesus Christ, a wish he often closes his epistles with (thus 1 Cor 16:23; 2 Cor 13:13; Col 4:18; 1 Thess 5:28; 2 Thess 3:18).

(16:21–23) A postscript adds greetings from Paul's companions. Some of the names are known to us from another quarter. Timothy is the fellow worker of Paul, well known from Paul's epistles (2 Cor 1:1; Phil 1:1; Col 1:1; 1 Thess 1:1; 2 Thess 1:1 Philemon 1) and from the Acts of the Apostles (16:1 et al.), whom Paul esteems very highly (16:21). Gaius is Paul's host in Corinth, a wealthy man whose hospitable house stands open to all Christians (16:23). Even Tertius, the scribe of the epistle, is allowed to immortalize himself with a greeting (16:22).

3   GLORIFICATION OF GOD

16: 25–27

16:25 Glory be to God who is able to strengthen you in accordance with the Good News I preach, which heralds Jesus, the Messiah, and reveals the mystery which has been kept hidden through eternal ages,

26 but which is now made known by the prophetical writings and proclaimed, by the command of the eternal God, to the Gentiles, so as to bring about their submission to the faith,

27 yes, to God, who alone is wise, be glory through Jesus Christ for ever and ever. Amen.

The epistle finally closes with a glorification of God and of his mystery. The three verses 16:25–27 form a single artistic sentence which is both a solemn confession of faith and a liturgical hymn.

(16:25) God is praised as the Powerful One who is capable of fulfilling the wish expressed: the prayer that follows. May God strengthen Christians in all dangers by the power which he reveals and gives! How this revelation takes place is described in three deepening levels and circles. It is directly present in the address by apostolic preaching, thus in the gospel of Paul (first level). Paul's preaching passes on the message of Jesus Christ (second level). The message of Christ comes out of the depth of God's mystery (third level). From the very beginning this mystery was concealed and hidden.

(16:26) But now God's mystery is revealed by the gospel of Christ and made known to all peoples according to the will of God in order to lead them to the saving obedience of faith. It is true that this mystery now revealed is already contained in the old Scriptures of the prophets. Its sense now reveals itself to the true, that is, the Christian interpretation. Paul himself practices this interpretation in many passages of the Epistle to the Romans in that he explains and shows from the words of the Old Testament how God's eternal plan of salvation is now being fulfilled in accordance with them.

(16:27) God's wisdom is wonderfully revealed in this plan of salvation embracing all times and peoples. Next to God's wisdom all other shrewdness disappears. He is the one and only wise God. Man bows before him in faith and adoration. To him belongs all honor and glory from the beginning to the end of all time, world without end.

As in 16:25 a verb is usually lacking in the New Testament glorifications of God (so also in 11:26). Should it be completed: to Him be glory, or: to Him is glory? We are accustomed to complete it in the former way ("Glory be to the Father . . ."). But it is questionable whether this completion is in accordance with the New Testament. Glory is not to be awarded to God in a prayer. He possesses his divine glory from all eternity and in all eternity. Man does not need to wish it; he can merely confess it.

But Christ is mentioned in the glorification as the mediator of the revelation of God to man and of the gratitude of man to God. Here as in other passages of the New Testament (2 Cor 1:20; Col 3:17; 1 Pet 4:11) the gratitude of the Church already rings out "through our Lord Jesus Christ, thy Son, who liveth and reigneth with thee, God world without end."

A comparison of style indicates several glorifications of God similar to 16:25–27 in the New Testament (Eph 3:20f; 1 Tim 1:17; Jude 24f) and in the literature which followed. In all these passages the tradition of Old Testament Jewish praise of God is used in the same way. But the style of 16:25–27 seems to distinguish itself from Paul's usual language in small details, yet clearly enough. With regard to the contents Paul's thoughts are certainly taken up (cf., for example, 11:33–36) but here and there they seem to be further developed. Thus a large part of modern exegesis tends toward the hypothesis that Paul himself is no longer speaking in these verses but rather a pupil of the apostle, a pupil who endorses and legitimizes the latter's gospel before the Church in the recognition and acknowledgment that the gospel of Christ's great apostle is the true word of Christ himself (16:25), and for the Church an inexhaustible abundance and an eternal, most precious treasure.

FOOTNOTES TO CHAPTER VI

[1] The wording and image of 15:16 recall Is 66:19f, where the prophet says: in the last age, in the messianic age of salvation, God's messengers will go out to all peoples and proclaim his glory everywhere. Jews and Gentiles will come in magnificent procession to the house of God as an offering for God. And God will appoint priests also from the Gentiles. In fact Paul fulfills the expectation and promise of later Jewish prophecy which is able to proclaim that the whole world will perceive and acknowledge the glory of Yahweh.

[2] For centuries Spain belonged to the Roman Empire and was covered with Roman roads and settlements from the coast far into the interior. Brisk trade existed between Rome and Spain and a journey to Spain was nothing out of the ordinary. There seems to have also been Jewish settlements there in New Testament times. The support which Paul could find in Rome might have consisted in a gift of money, but also in the provision of letters of recommendation or in escort by members of the Roman community. According to early Church tradition, testified to in the letter of the Roman Bishop Clemens (1 Clemens 5:5–7) from the year 96 and elsewhere, Paul did in fact carry out the journey to Spain.

[3] It seems in 15:26 that not a part of the saints is to be designated as the poor; but the saints can also be called the poor (as in Gal 2:10). In the texts recently come to light in Qumran the members of the community there call themselves both the saints and the poor.

[4] In Acts 20 it is reported how Paul carried out the journey planned from Corinth to Jerusalem according to Rom 15:25. In Miletus he interrupts the journey for a short time and sends for the elders of the community of Ephesus. Also before them he speaks of the threatening dangers (Acts 20:22f): "And now I am

going to Jerusalem under spiritual compulsion, not knowing what will happen to me there, except that in every city the Holy Spirit assures me that imprisonment and persecution are awaiting me."

[5] In verse 15:30 Christ, the Spirit and the Father, thus the Persons of the divine Trinity, are mentioned in one sentence, although not in the order familiar to us. Several such trinitarian formulas are found in the Pauline epistles (cf. 1 Cor 12:4–6; 2 Cor 13:13). The fundamental structure of Paul's thinking is trinitarian.

[6] Verse 16:24 is found in only a part of the manuscripts, and in the later manuscripts of the Epistle to the Romans at that. The verse seems to have been added later, and is then evidently a doubling of 16:20b.

[7] Exegesis discusses the question of whether Rom 16 is an original part of the Epistle to the Romans, or perhaps attached to it from another Pauline epistle. The oldest preserved manuscripts, including a papyrus from the third century, place the glorification 16:25–27 after 15:33 and conclude the epistle with chapter 15. To this external finding are added internal reasons taken from Rom 16 itself. One asks how Paul, in the city of Rome completely strange to him, is to know individually the many Christians whom he greets by name in 16:3–16. Prisca and Aquila, mentioned first in 16:3, live in Ephesus according to 1 Cor 16:19; 2 Tim 4:19; Acts 18:19, 26. Thus some supposed Rom 16 to be an original Epistle to the Ephesians or, since an epistle can hardly have consisted in greetings alone, at least a fragment of such an epistle. The greater part of exegesis today assumes nevertheless that Rom 16 is the genuine conclusion of the Epistle to the Romans. The ancient manuscripts mentioned may have left out Rom 16 because they considered the list of greetings unimportant. Prisca and Aquila may have emigrated from Ephesus to Rome. With the multitudinous travel in the Mediterranean world of that time it is easily possible that so many Christians, become well known to Paul in the east, had in the meantime migrated to Rome. Paul may perhaps have enumerated them all individually in order to recommend to the community, which did not know him, to inquire about him of those mentioned.